In a technologically driven world where ends increasingly justify means, this book offers some perspective *before* you get stuck in the rat race. The rhythms we default to at the start of our working lives ⌐⌐ ⌐ for better or worse, and with *Final*, you job of it than I did!
Andy Flannagan, Director CSM

Finishing uni was a traumatic life chang navigate my way into the next phase of insightful, practically working through ⌐ ⌐⌐ ⌐o studentdom and hello to the big bad world!
Andy Frost, Share Jesus International

I love the way Krish writes: he hooks you and then pulls you in, and you find such priceless wisdom and guidance. He is robust and clear about how we should shape our priorities around our calling to be God's recruits, whether that is as a city banker, a world-renowned medical researcher or a youth worker. It is all part of God's mission. Every church should hand out this book to uni graduates en masse, because it contains the kind of wisdom, support and clarity that young adults in our churches often feel starved of.
Rachel Gardner, Romance Academy

Bite-sized, but thought-provoking. Worth using, either as a health check or to lay down valuable markers for Christian discipleship.
Hugh Palmer, All Souls, Langham Place

Finishing university and starting work can be a stressful and confusing time, but Krish helps sort through the pressures and steers the reader back to God. *Final* contains loads of practical advice, from how to navigate the job application process to how to keep focused on God and bringing his kingdom; I believe this book will provide invaluable direction and help for many.
Mike Pilavachi, Soul Survivor

I remember my final year at uni very well, and have so much sympathy for everyone now going through it themselves. *Final* plugs a much-needed gap, and I know it will prove to be a lifeline for many students. Krish writes so well, holding together the biblical and the practical in a really helpful way, and his wealth of experience and wisdom shines through on every page. I know I shall be buying this book for my nieces and nephews in years to come!
Ruth Valerio, Manager of A Rocha's Living Lightly project

Krish Kandiah

final

**Bite-sized inspiration
for final-year students**

ivp

INTER-VARSITY PRESS
Norton Street, Nottingham NG7 3HR, England
Email: ivp@ivpbooks.com
Website: www.ivpbooks.com

First published 2010

British Library Cataloguing in Publication Data
A catalogue record for this book is available from the British Library.

ISBN: 978–1–84474–445–9

Set in 10/12.5pt Calibri
Typeset in Great Britain by CRB Associates, Potterhanworth, Lincolnshire
Printed in Great Britain by Ashford Colour Press Ltd, Gosport, Hampshire

Inter-Varsity Press publishes Christian books that are true to the Bible and that communicate the gospel, develop discipleship and strengthen the church for its mission in the world.

Inter-Varsity Press is closely linked with the Universities and Colleges Christian Fellowship, a student movement connecting Christian Unions in universities and colleges throughout Great Britain, and a member movement of the International Fellowship of Evangelical Students. Website: www.uccf.org.uk

My son, do not forget my teaching,
   but keep my commands in your heart,
for they will prolong your life many years
   and bring you prosperity.
Let love and faithfulness never leave you;
   bind them around your neck,
   write them on the tablet of your heart.
Then you will win favour and a good name
   in the sight of God and humankind.
Trust in the Lord with all your heart
   and lean not on your own understanding;
in all your ways acknowledge him,
   and he will make your paths straight.
(Proverbs 3:1-6)

Finally . . . I had my life all mapped out. After sleepless nights, countless discussions with careers advisors, parents and mentors, I knew exactly what I was going to do with my life. Finally I had an answer to the question that people seemed to be asking me every five minutes. I could now tell them I was destined to get a first-class chemistry degree and become a world-renowned medicinal researcher in communist Russia, where I would also live as an undercover evangelist and a dedicated bachelor missionary until the day I was martyred for my faith.

It was a great plan. I worked harder than ever in lectures and labs; I took a Russian language module and visited Moscow each holiday, even wangling a free trip out of the university exchange programme. But just as my dream was within reach, disaster struck on several fronts. Firstly, the harder I worked, the more I discovered chemistry for me was intellectual torture, sucking the will to live out of me and dooming me to a below average quali-fication. Secondly, the Iron Curtain fell and missionaries without any science degrees whatsoever were pouring into 'my' mission field. Thirdly, I fell in love, bringing with it the added complications of somebody else's dreams and smashing my dedication to bachelorhood. And fourthly, I had the nagging feeling that God was teaching me not only that the world did not revolve around me, but that he wanted to do something different with my life. So I found myself lost, halfway through my final year at university, facing the abyss of an unknown and rapidly impending future.

It was at this point that I realized my peers were dividing into distinct groups. First of all, there were the laid-back students who were not worried about life after finals because, like me a week earlier, they believed they had it all mapped out, or because they were having too much fun – or too much stress

– in the moment to worry. They were content just to cruise through the final year and into their future. Secondly, there were the starry-eyed students who believed the world was their oyster and that they were as likely to be bungee jumping off the Golden Gate Bridge in twelve months' time as to be sitting in their penthouse office, having landed that cushy job with the six-figure salary.

But now that my dream job was as far removed from planet Earth as the Sputnik, and just as obsolete, I had to come to terms with the fact that I was part of the rapidly growing third group of finalists – those who were running around the campus like headless chickens, panicking that they would make the wrong decision, fail their exams and end up living back home with their mothers and their Spiderman or Barbie doll duvets.

FINAL is born out of my own stomach-churning months of the final year as I juggled exams, interviews, relationships, Christian faith and career decisions. I have been encouraged along the way by the input of other finalists with their different questions, hopes and fears – and quotations! But mostly this book is shaped by the Bible – our guide to the whole of life. *FINAL* will not tell you what career path to choose, but like a Sat Nav, it may be able to help you programme in your final destination, as well as suggest a variety of routes, avoid roadblocks and speed traps, and point out some useful landmarks along the way.

Finally . . . as we start out on this journey together, I am inspired by the only prayer Jesus taught his disciples to pray – a prayer that teaches us not to fear the future but to long for it: 'Your kingdom come, your will be done, on earth as it is in heaven' (Matthew 6:10).

ents

week 1

Facing your future

Monday:
Career

Tuesday:
Ambition

Wednesday:
Qualifications

Thursday:
Security

Friday:
Workplace

Saturday:
Reward

Sunday:
Boss

> And why do you worry about clothes? See how the flowers of the field grow. They do not labour or spin. Yet I tell you that not even Solomon in all his splendour was dressed like one of these. If that is how God clothes the grass of the field, which is here today and tomorrow is thrown into the fire, will he not much more clothe you – you of little faith? So do not worry, saying, 'What shall we eat?' or 'What shall we drink?' or 'What shall we wear?' For the pagans run after all these things, and your heavenly Father knows that you need them. But seek first his kingdom and his righteousness, and all these things will be given to you as well. Therefore do not worry about tomorrow, for tomorrow will worry about itself. Each day has enough trouble of its own.
>
> (Matthew 6:28–34)

The love triangle was tearing the East London lad apart. He was engaged to be married to his childhood sweetheart, Mandy, but recently he had become besotted with Maria from the office. He was plagued by the dilemma – should he dump Mandy so he could have Maria, or forget the girl of his dreams, and stick with his soulmate? Some of his friends pushed him one direction, others gave the totally opposite advice. Eventually he decided to ask God himself for guidance. He walked into a Catholic church near his house and prayed: ''Ello God, 'ere's the thing – 'oo should I choose – Mandy or Maria?' He looked up and on the wall he saw his answer as clear as day – 'Ave Maria'. The lad skipped out, confident that his decision had been rubber-stamped by the Almighty himself – and promptly broke off his engagement.

Wouldn't it be great to have specific and unmistakable guidance from God – especially during the final year of university when we can become overwhelmed with the magnitude and multitude of decisions in front of us? What sort of job should I apply for? Where should I live? Should I do more studies? Should I propose? Should I travel the world? Should I write my CV or my dissertation? What happens if it all goes horribly wrong? Our brains can easily begin to feel like a computer that has too many programmes running at once and is on the verge of crashing, and our natural instinct is to shut down. Just like the lad in the story, we will go to any length to find answers. But the poor boy had no more heard guidance from God than the girl who, looking for careers advice, randomly opened her Bible and read, 'The tablets were the work of God' (Exodus 32:16) and decided to become a pharmacist, or the guy who read, 'Serve the food' (Genesis 43:31) and became a waiter!

Does this mean the Bible has nothing to say about careers advice and life-changing decisions? Absolutely not – the Bible has a lot of wisdom to offer about all our plans, and there is one passage that is relevant to every Christian beginning to consider, or worry about, their future. It contains a decision on which all other decisions hang: are we going to 'seek first God's kingdom'?

1. Seeking God's kingdom means a change of priorities

Imagine I was to fill a large glass jar with the entire contents of a tray full of sand, pebbles and rocks. If I began with the sand and the pebbles, the chances of manoeuvring the rocks in at the end would be slim – there would simply be no space left. The best strategy would be to put the largest objects in first and then add the pebbles and sand afterwards. In the same way, we need to make sure that big things in our lives are sorted first and allow everything else to fit in around them. Too often God's kingship gets crowded out of our lives by the insignificant, so God tells us to make sure that his kingdom is the priority in our lives and to let details such as career prospects and income, clothing and food fit in afterwards. In these first seven days we want to put the rocks into the jar. We might feel that the other topics in this book are more urgent, but unless we take heed of the important challenge to seek God's kingdom first, it is possible that there will simply not be enough space in our lives to seek God's kingdom at all.

2. Seeking God's kingdom means a change of principles

Putting God's agenda first means that our primary job is to be God's recruit in the world, whatever our career or salary or location. Jesus' words are to people who have no idea where their next meal is coming from or how they will replace the clothes on their back when they wear thin. However low our bank accounts get, however bleak the job market seems, however insurmountable our student debts feel, we are rarely fearful that we will starve or be made homeless. Nevertheless, if Jesus can command the poorest people to prioritize building the kingdom over their own worries and plans, then we too should work out how to get stuck into God's kingdom agenda before we start worrying about other life decisions.

When we decide to prioritize our life in this way, Jesus promises that God will take care of all our needs. Does this mean we can close the book now and sit back and watch God come through on his promise? No more than the birds of the air can wait in their nests for worms and berries to be served on a plate, or the grass of the field can give up shooting roots and order a still mineral water with ice and lemon. With the decision to seek first God's kingdom firmly established, we can be reassured that God will provide for us. Then we can work out how to use our skills and abilities to access the resources and plans he has available for us.

In this passage how does Jesus rightly disturb the comfortable and comfort the disturbed. Which camp do you tend to fall into and how can you move to centre ground?

 Further study: Compare the verses above, Jesus' challenge to the poor (18–34), with the preceding verses (19–24), Jesus' challenge to the rich. Why is prioritizing God's kingdom not career suicide?

 Prayer: Meditate for four minutes on the four words of Jesus' command: 'Seek first God's kingdom.' Write down what God might be saying to you through each one.

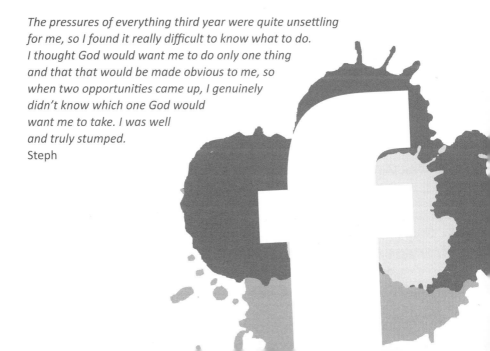

The pressures of everything third year were quite unsettling for me, so I found it really difficult to know what to do. I thought God would want me to do only one thing and that that would be made obvious to me, so when two opportunities came up, I genuinely didn't know which one God would want me to take. I was well and truly stumped.
Steph

> Then I saw 'a new heaven and a new earth,' for the first heaven and the first earth had passed away, and there was no longer any sea. I saw the Holy City, the new Jerusalem, coming down out of heaven from God, prepared as a bride beautifully dressed for her husband. And I heard a loud voice from the throne saying, 'Look! God's dwelling-place is now among the people, and he will dwell with them. They will be his people, and God himself will be with them and be their God. "He will wipe every tear from their eyes. There will be no more death" or mourning or crying or pain, for the old order of things has passed away.'
> (Revelation 21:1–4)

It looked like a tornado had hit my house. Bits of tiles and plaster were littering the room, rusting cabinets were ripped off the walls and there was dust everywhere. But this was no natural disaster. It wasn't even my student accommodation! This was payback time. As I wielded the sledgehammer, I am sure old Mrs Delamura was turning in her grave. It was once, no doubt, the peak of kitchen design and her pride and joy, befitting the ambitious West London ice-cream maker. But the colour of vomit just did not go with my culinary tastes, and my ambitions for my work, lifestyle and family did not include fifty-year-old dirt. So with my IKEA catalogue and its promise of perfect gleaming kitchens for inspiration, the demolition began.

There is a hint in Revelation 21 that my old kitchen is not unlike our world. Once immaculate, God's perfect creation, pride and joy, it is now the place of death, mourning, crying and pain. It is time for a major refurbishment, and this passage inspires us with a glimpse of what God is planning for his kingdom, and how our ambitions fit into the grand scheme of things.

1. God's creation

Unlike the sledgehammer approach I took to removing my old kitchen before installing the new one, God has a very different plan for his creation. The word 'new' in this passage means 'restored' or 'revitalized', not unlike an artist removing the grime from a dusty canvas to reveal the original masterpiece. God is not planning to take us away to a brand new, purpose-built planet; he plans to renovate everything we see around us.

2. God's company

Whenever major bands came to gig at my university, I played paparazzi to see if I could get an autograph or even a conversation with some of my musical heroes. I would get out my best clothes, and even tidy my room on the off chance they would stop by. But my hopes were always dashed, as it was very difficult to get close enough even to say hello. But when God comes, he promises that we will have full access to his company. He is not coming to perform or to be worshipped from a distance. He is not popping down for a half-hour walkabout. Revelation 21 is clear that God is coming to move in with us.

3. God's community

God reveals the ultimate plot spoiler for the entire story of history through a man in enforced exile writing to a ridiculed minority group facing persecution from Jewish and Roman leaders. Through the book of Revelation, God lets his people know that at the end of history they would not be sent to live on personal clouds in the uninterrupted silence of eternal space, but they would live in the hustle and bustle of a multicultural city. This city is God's church, which he describes as his centrepiece, the bride with whom he and we will live happily ever after.

God's plans for the future revolve around his creation and his church enjoying his company. This vision should shape the way we live every day and our own plans for the future; otherwise we are in danger of spending our lives building sandcastles on the beach when the tide is coming in.

Ambition can be a destructive force. It can blind us to God's big picture and his guidance in our lives. It can sledgehammer its way through relationships and principles in order to achieve its goal, whatever the cost. But ambition can also be constructive. By seeking first God's kingdom, our own ambitions for our work, our lifestyle and our family should slot in with God's ambitions for the creation, for the church and for our community.

This passage reminds me of my favourite football match of all time – the Champions League Final Liverpool v. AC Milan played in Istanbul in 2005. I'd invited all my friends to watch it on a big screen in my front lounge. At half-time we were down 3–0, and most of my guests gave up and went home. But then followed one of football's most amazing comebacks worthy of the team I had loyally supported for twenty years. The discouragement of the first half only served to make the final victory even sweeter. When we look around at our earth, at our church and at our lives, making our ambition in life to seek first God's kingdom may seem like a lost cause. It is difficult to believe that God can turn it all around to bring victory out of apparent defeat. Yet taking time to consider our true champion's promised comeback can motivate us to keep our selfish desires in check and stay ambitious for God's kingdom.

Write down three practical ideas you could incorporate into your life to demonstrate how you could work on valuing your relationship with God, your environment and your church.

Ambitions for my relationship with God	Ambitions for my environment	Ambitions for my church

 Further study: Take a closer look at Genesis 1 – 2. What similarities and differences do you see in God's original intention for humanity and how things end up in Revelation 21?

 Prayer: Spend some time meditating on a world without death, mourning, crying and pain, and make a covenant with God to spend your life preparing yourself and others for that place.

Even after all I had learned about myself at uni, it still wasn't clear what kind of job God had made me for. I knew I was pretty well organized, but I didn't find my first admin job satisfying enough. I realized that God had made me to be more of a 'people-person' and so I ended up entering the world of Human Resources, which combined my organizational skills with lots of personal interaction. Alex

> Praise be to the God and Father of our Lord Jesus Christ, who has blessed us in the heavenly realms with every spiritual blessing in Christ. For he chose us in him before the creation of the world to be holy and blameless in his sight. In love he predestined us for adoption to sonship through Jesus Christ, in accordance with his pleasure and will – to the praise of his glorious grace, which he has freely given us in the One he loves. In him we have redemption through his blood, the forgiveness of sins, in accordance with the riches of God's grace that he lavished on us. With all wisdom and understanding, he made known to us the mystery of his will according to his good pleasure, which he purposed in Christ, to be put into effect when the times reach their fulfilment – to bring unity to all things in heaven and on earth under Christ.
> (Ephesians 1:3–10)

Relationships in the first term of each university year seem to demonstrate the accuracy of the second law of thermodynamics, which basically states that eventually everything disintegrates. In student communities, relationships blossom then break down, and arguments ensue over whether the guy was a creep or the girl was cheap. Then the factions happen. There is the 'let's-cook-together' crowd versus the 'don't-touch-my-space-in-the-fridge' contingent. There is the 'artsy-students-are-where-it's-at' gang versus the 'scientists-are-the-only-real-students' mob, and things just get messier from there on in.

When I watch the news I see that international relations are just as fragile and that factions seem to be an inevitable part of human existence, and yet the Bible promises a very different future. This passage, like yesterday's, points to the fact that one day Jesus will rule supreme over a reconciled and unified universe. Most people would love to be in on this but feel they have to earn their way in. They often do this through trying to live a good life, making a significant contribution to their society, being a good neighbour or trying to make the most of the life they have been given.

The Bible is very clear that there is only one way we can be part of God's eternal kingdom, and this chapter lists the qualifications we need to get there. But all these qualifications are tied in, not to what we have achieved, but to what Jesus has achieved for us.

Jesus the Saviour

I didn't like being a graduand. It was that strange waiting period between discovering that I had amazingly passed my chemistry degree and that qualification being conferred formally at my graduation ceremony. I felt I had earned my qualification, no matter what anybody else said or did. This passage shows us God's order of things, and it turns our normal ways of thinking upside down. First of all, even before the creation of the world, we are conferred with the qualifications as listed in this chapter – forgiveness, grace, reconciliation, adoption, wisdom. These qualifications come without any lectures, labs or library time – without having to do any essays or exams. At Jesus' expense, they are given freely to us. Then comes the waiting period before we are ceremonially welcomed into God's visible presence. Paul's response to this generous grace is typical of grateful Christians who don't wait around passively, but in private and in public are full of prayer and praise.

Jesus the Lord

In the rest of this letter Paul goes on to talk about two other hallmarks of the active lives of Christians. The first is unity: because we have put our hope and trust in Jesus and all he has done for us, we have something unique in common with all Christians everywhere and we are drawn together. The second is integrity: one day everything, as well as everyone, will be put under Jesus' control, and so we choose to live now following the lordship of Jesus in every aspect of our lives. These two hallmarks give the people around us a glimpse of God's future now, just as a movie trailer grabs our attention by showing snapshots of the best bits of the upcoming film.

The great news for us is that if history is destined to be resolved in Jesus, and if we follow him, our story ends well – not that we chose well, but rather that God chose us well; not that we bring any qualifications of our own, but that Jesus qualifies us. These truths free us from basing our identity, our sense of self-worth, our acceptance or our purpose in life on gaining earthly qualifications. These truths also free us to do our best and work hard at our earthly qualifications as part of our worship and service to God.

 Just as a qualified doctor can't just sit back and watch when he's on the scene of an accident, so we cannot expect our Christian lives to be passive. To what extent are our lives hallmarked by active private and public prayer and praise? To what extent are our lives characterized by unity and integrity? How does this make a practical difference in our fractured community?

Further study: Read the whole letter to the Ephesians in one sitting. Make a note of all the places where Paul mentions the free qualification of grace, and the challenges actively to live that out in prayer and praise, or in unity and integrity.

 Prayer: Write out your own 'Praise be . . . ' prayer in recognition of all that God has qualified you with.

I had already volunteered with Scripture Union for a regular annual youth mission in the town, so I instinctively helped out with the Saltmine team. We got chatting and I was challenged to think about applying for some new evangelism teams they were setting up. I laughed it off initially though. I think I felt I needed to be a spiritual giant, which I wasn't/am not! To cut it short, a postgraduate business qualification evolved into children's evangelism! Almost twenty years later I became Head of Missions – arguably finally combining business and management with children's evangelism.
Alan

In him we were also chosen, having been predestined according to the plan of him who works out everything in conformity with the purpose of his will, in order that we, who were the first to put our hope in Christ, might be for the praise of his glory. And you also were included in Christ when you heard the word of truth, the gospel of your salvation. When you believed, you were marked in him with a seal, the promised Holy Spirit, who is a deposit guaranteeing our inheritance until the redemption of those who are God's possession – to the praise of his glory.

For this reason, ever since I heard about your faith in the Lord Jesus and your love for all his people, I have not stopped giving thanks for you, remembering you in my prayers. I keep asking that the God of our Lord Jesus Christ, the glorious Father, may give you the Spirit of wisdom and revelation, so that you may know him better. I pray that the eyes of your heart may be enlightened in order that you may know the hope to which he has called you, the riches of his glorious inheritance in his people, and his incomparably great power for us who believe. That power is the same as the mighty strength he exerted when he raised Christ from the dead and seated him at his right hand in the heavenly realms, far above all rule and authority, power and dominion, and every name that can be invoked, not only in the present age but also in the one to come. (Ephesians 1:11–21)

Kyle began university with a determination to share his faith, live out his faith and grow in his faith. During the next three years he won many of his friends to Christ, and gained the respect of the Christians around him. He took a year out to work for the church before embarking on a career in teaching. But three years later Kyle was reported by his university friends as 'missing in action'. He hadn't been seen in a church for several months. Had he been captured by opposing forces or wounded in action, or had he in fact deserted the faith he had once clung to so hard?

Many Christians leave university and are quickly distracted by the call of the world, get burnt out by the demands of the church, or grow tired of fighting the good fight. Although job security is increasingly a factor in choosing a career, security in our faith needs to be a major consideration in our choices. This passage offers us three assurances that, as we make decisions about faith and our future, God is there to hold us to them.

1. Chosen by God

I am hoping my daughter will never be teased at school because she is adopted. But in case of such a playground emergency, I want her to have this quick one-line defence up her sleeve: 'At least *my* parents *chose* me.' We often refer to following Jesus as our personal decision. However, the Bible speaks very differently about our conversion. Paul here reminds the Ephesians that their faith is no accident or whim or phase we are going through, but that God initiated it. He knew us and chose us, and he adopted us and predestined us for the 'praise of *his* glory'. Our faith security is *his* business.

2. Confirmed by the Holy Spirit

The Holy Spirit's presence in our lives is God's down payment on us. The moment we believe, God the Holy Spirit takes up residence within us. His presence guarantees that God will deliver on all of his promises to us all the way through to eternity. What better security could we have than God himself living in us?

3. Connected to Jesus

On its own, a laptop can access only the resources installed on its hard drive, but when it connects to a wireless network the whole of the web's resources suddenly become available. Paul's strange phrase 'in Christ' repeated six times in this chapter reminds us that our faith connects us to God's big plan for the universe and all the resources Jesus has to offer.

Our security as Christians is countersigned by God the Father, God the Son and God the Holy Spirit. When we are feeling least confident about the future and wondering whether our faith will be derailed by debt, doubt or disappointment, we can be reassured by Paul's words that God the Holy Trinity's commitment to us cannot be defeated, even by the greatest powers of death, demons or other dominions. Rejection, redundancy and recession cannot separate us from the power of God.

 How does being secure in our faith help us when facing other insecurities in life? Think of what you would say to the following people in light of today's passage:

'I'm such an insecure person, I don't think I'll ever trust anybody again.'

'My job is on the line and I don't know how I will pay my mortgage next month.'

'I've only been a Christian a month and my faith is too fragile to cope with life outside university.'

Further study: Many Christians wonder how they can be sure the Holy Spirit is really resident in them and there to stay. What do the following passages teach us about this? Galatians 5, Romans 8, 1 Corinthians 12, Ephesians 1.

 Prayer: Ask God to help you take in the reassurances he offers. Ask him to help you grow in the areas of wisdom, revelation, enlightenment, hope and the riches of our inheritance.

Following the suggestion that I might be made redundant from the company I'd worked for for twenty-eight years, I swung between disbelief and anger at the shallowness of the company's decision. God led me back to some daily reading material from eight years ago with the poignant theme of being led into the desert. I found this a hard lesson and to a degree I still do, but it was essential for me to refocus my attention on God.
Mark

> By faith Abraham, when called to go to a place he would later receive as his inheritance, obeyed and went, even though he did not know where he was going. By faith he made his home in the promised land like a stranger in a foreign country; he lived in tents, as did Isaac and Jacob, who were heirs with him of the same promise. For he was looking forward to the city with foundations, whose architect and builder is God. And by faith even Sarah, who was past child-bearing age, was enabled to bear children because she considered him faithful who had made the promise. And so from this one man, and he as good as dead, came descendants as numerous as the stars in the sky and as countless as the sand on the seashore.
>
> All these people were still living by faith when they died. They did not receive the things promised; they only saw them and welcomed them from a distance, admitting that they were foreigners and strangers on earth. People who say such things show that they are looking for a country of their own. If they had been thinking of the country they had left, they would have had opportunity to return. Instead, they were longing for a better country – a heavenly one. Therefore God is not ashamed to be called their God, for he has prepared a city for them.
>
> (Hebrews 11:8–16)

They had no idea where they were going. My friend loves to live life on the edge and has an eye for a bargain, and so each year he leaves it until the very last moment and then books a last-minute deal for a holiday. I have a mental picture of his family at the check-in desk with fur coats and bikinis, snorkel gear and skis. I wonder if his kids have a sparkle in their eyes as they wonder what delights they will see, or if they are in a strop wishing they could stay at home and play Xbox? As they got in the car to the airport that morning, no-one had a clue how to answer their question, 'are we nearly there yet?'

When God relocated Abraham he was not told where he was going or how long it would take to get there.

1. Where we are called to live will not always seem the logical option

When God called Abraham to leave safety, security, business and family, and step off the map, I can just imagine how his friends would have reacted: 'But this is a huge risk. What about all the assets you have worked so hard for here? And you have no back-up plan? You don't even speak the language. At twenty years old perhaps – but at ninety?! You must be mad!' Abraham must have felt God was sending him in totally the wrong direction. He should have been settling down for retirement, not setting off with a one-way ticket. He should have been worrying about his burial arrangements, not his baby's birth plans. He should have been talking about the good old days in the past, not the prospect of discovering cities and countries in the future. But God's call on our lives is often counter-intuitive, and faith is always an adventure into the unknown, as we trust God wherever he leads us.

2. Where we are going is less important than whom we are following

Abraham was not told where he was to go to, but he knew what he was called to do. He was going to trust, obey and follow God, and be a blessing to the people he would meet, drawing them to his God. In the New Testament, we see a parallel when Jesus asked a bunch of fishermen to follow him. They did not know their destination, but they were sure of their vocation. Like them, we are to trust and follow Jesus and, like soldiers who undergo training without knowing where they may be deployed, we are to join him in his mission.

3. Where we live in the short-term is less important than where we are going to live in the long-term

Abraham knew that wherever he pitched his tent, his days of camping were numbered. Eventually he knew that he would be living with God in a place that wouldn't wear out, leak or blow away. Jesus too was unconcerned about housing and belongings, because he knew his ultimate destination was to be back with his Father. Whether we fancy living in a luxury pad in the city, a hut on a beach, or a country cottage, we should remember it is just a stopover on our way to eternity. Abraham was homesick, we were told, not for the home he had left behind, but for the home he had not yet reached.

Abraham had to wait a long time to see God's promises to him fulfilled. The child, the nation, the land and the blessings were not delivered by first-class mail the moment he stepped out of Ur. It took him the whole of his lifetime to see God's plan working out. It was Abraham's confident trust in the fact that God knew best that enabled him to choose to live in the place God had chosen for him.

 Talk to two senior Christians about how God has led them, and how differently their lives turned out from what they expected when they were twenty. Where in the world would *you* choose to live, and how prepared are you to let God choose for you?

Further study: Go back to Genesis 12 to read the story of Abraham. Find the 'crossroads' moments in his story and see how he made his choices.

 Prayer: Thank God that wherever you go in this world, you will never be alone. Read Psalm 139 as a prayer to God.

Throughout uni my faith was tested, torn and rebuilt, and leaving uni was great because it meant the next step in this journey with God, and really there's nothing better than moving forward with and in him. My only advice is to consider his call and purpose for your life, rather than the next sensible step for career or comfort. You never know where he might lead you, and that's the greatest place to be in his hands, despite the uncertainty you might feel as you step into the unknown.
Dave

Therefore, since we are surrounded by such a great cloud of witnesses, let us throw off everything that hinders and the sin that so easily entangles. And let us run with perseverance the race marked out for us, fixing our eyes on Jesus, the pioneer and perfecter of faith. For the joy that was set before him he endured the cross, scorning its shame, and sat down at the right hand of the throne of God. Consider him who endured such opposition from sinners, so that you will not grow weary and lose heart. (Hebrews 12:1–3)

I was very hungry, and just as my stomach growled at me for the tenth time, I saw the gleaming golden arches of a drive-thru restaurant in the distance. The prospect of a burger or a piece of fried chicken silenced my stomach and made my lips water. The restaurant got closer and a glowing sign invited me to take the next turning on the right. Over the mounds of packaging, I could see the people inside eating. I could see the spaces in the car park and feel the coins burning through my pockets. Then I watched it all disappear through my rear-view mirror. Ahead of me the ambulance I was following put on its siren as it sped through the traffic lights. Inside it was my two-year-old son, and the only place I was going to that night was the hospital, no matter how hungry I was.

If I had been on the way to the library to do some revision, or on my way to the gym to work out, then I would have been far more easily distracted. But on this occasion there was no stopping me. I kept my eyes fixed on the ambulance as it took me on an unknown route through an unknown city, because getting treatment for my son was a reward worth any sacrifice. In this passage we see that we must refuse to be distracted by anything that might hinder us from pursuing Jesus, with all its rewards and sacrifices.

The writer to the Hebrews tells us that there are several things that might mean we lose sight of Jesus. We might get held back by life's paraphernalia, entangled by sin, wearied from opposition, or even give up before the end. The picture he uses is of an athlete, and just as a runner improves step by step by developing speed, stamina and strength, we too can use these ideas to take a closer look at what the end reward should inspire us to do.

Speed

Some male athletes go through the embarrassment of shaving their legs in an effort to shave microseconds off their time, and this dedication to dump unnecessary baggage will help us avoid delays in our faith journey. Jesus taught us how to run light and be ruthless with sin and temptation as he focused on the cross. As we go through key decision-making periods in our life, it may be time to check what baggage may be causing us to lose focus. Just as many of us need training buddies or pacemakers to help us run to our maximum speed, so it might be helpful to ask a friend to pray with us, and ask us tough questions as we decide on our next step.

Stamina

I was proud of the fact that I used to run the 100-metre sprint at school, until I met Patsy who has completed seventy-three marathons in the last three years and is still counting. She has helped me see that the Christian life is more like a marathon than a sprint. A quick burst of energy and rapid spiritual growth in as short a time as possible will just not help us last the race. Jesus calls us to endure for the long haul and offers himself as our pioneer, pacesetter and perfecter. The path Jesus takes us on is the path of the cross, a way of pain and shame, and many of the decisions we make will be difficult, as some of us have already experienced. I like the way Eugene Peterson describes the development of character in this way as 'a long obedience in the same direction' (Eugene H. Peterson, *A Long Obedience in the Same Direction*, InterVarsity Press, 2000).

Strength

Just as runners build up their strength by alternating workouts and rest days, reflection time in our faith is as significant as action time. As our schedule gets busier with project deadlines, essays and then exams, taking time out to check we are still on course is vital. Many Christians put this into practice by making space for listening to God and enjoying time with his people, or by adopting the discipline of Sabbath and working six days out of seven. This not only strengthens our relationship with God, but also strengthens us to serve him better during the rest of the week.

Step by step

As we look ahead to the marathon that God has laid in front of us, we can't see the whole route, let alone the finish line. Nevertheless, God asks us to commit the rest of our lives to him and to run the long race with him. As we look towards the future, we may feel we have to make decisions about our entire life, although often God guides us one life step at a time. But God's marathon is designed with each step to bring us closer to the reward that is already prepared for us.

Pay cheques, perks and promotions are the rewards that motivate many people around us, but if we have ever followed an ambulance containing a loved one in critical condition, we know that those things are little more meaningful than a Big Mac. When faced with real pain, real decisions and real reward, our only hope is to travel life step by step with Jesus, enjoying the rewards along the way, but refusing to let them distract us from reaching out to gain the ultimate reward at the end.

 Using the headings 'Speed', 'Stamina' and 'Strength', put together a plan to run the marathon of faith that will help you to progress, to persevere and to endure. How can you make sure your eternal rewards motivate you over and above your earning potential?

 Further study: If Hebrews 12 inspires us from the starting block, 2 Timothy 4 inspires us from the finish line. Note the differences and the similarities.

 Prayer: Ask God to show you what may drag you backwards in your journey of faith, and what may help you move forwards.

Going into your last year at uni feels like going into the last lap of a long race – let's say an egg and spoon race.
You know it's going to feel great to finish,
but you're worried that when it's all over
you're just going to be left standing
there with a spoon and an egg.
Then you're expected to go
and make a life for yourself.
Ben

> Again, it will be like a man going on a journey, who called his servants and entrusted his wealth to them. To one he gave five bags of gold, to another two bags, and to another one bag, each according to his ability. Then he went on his journey. The man who had received five bags of gold went at once and put his money to work and gained five bags more. So also, the one with two bags of gold gained two more. But the man who had received one bag went off, dug a hole in the ground and hid his master's money.
>
> After a long time the master of those servants returned and settled accounts with them.
>
> (Matthew 25:14–19)

He was late and I was annoyed. It was rush hour so there was a constant stream of comings and goings at the north exit of Baker Street station. Time was dragging as I waited for my friend to turn up. I took pen and paper out of my backpack and started jotting down some ideas for a sermon I had to give at the weekend. Occasionally I would look around searching for my appointment in the crowd, and then go back to my scribbles. After twenty minutes a policeman wandered over. Somebody had reported a terror suspect in the vicinity making copious notes on the activities at Baker Street tube station. I glanced around nervously before realizing that the suspicious dark-skinned loiterer with the bulging backpack was in fact me!

Waiting is a dangerous occupation. Not only because others may fail to understand our actions, but also because over time our priorities can change. Jesus' parable illustrates that waiting can make us forget who we are waiting for and who we are working for. It is sandwiched between two other parables about waiting: the story of the ten virgins highlights the fact that it could be a long wait and we need to make long-range plans so that we don't neglect our duties. The second parable, the story of the sheep and the goats, reminds us to treat those around us well while we are waiting. But this parable of the talents is particularly pertinent to those of us who are facing decisions about our future. It asks us to consider three things as we wait for Jesus to return.

1. God recruits us

Working in an open-plan office is supposed to engender greater concentration and productivity for the simple reason that people work harder when they know their boss can see them. But God is not the sort of boss that breathes down our necks, piles on the pressures and makes impossible demands on us. We have already seen that we don't need to work to earn our way into God's good books. But we can easily forget that the one we call Saviour and friend is also our Lord and master. Jesus is the one we work for, and as we consider our future options, he should shape our decisions above parental expectations, peer pressure or marketeering propaganda.

2. God respects us

God delegates responsibilities to his church and gives each of us resources to work in his family business. In the ancient world a talent was a large sum of money, representing something like twenty years of a day labourer's wages. God trusts us with an enormous amount and variety of resources – time, energy, talents, gifts and opportunities. God also has given us a huge amount of freedom according to this parable. We are not given a manual prescribing exactly what to do and when. Instead we are allowed to exercise our own creativity and make our own choices about what best to do with what God has given us. Many people hope God will give them a perfect blueprint for their lives but most of the time God does not operate in this way. This is not because God is delegating jobs he doesn't want to do himself. God wants to develop our maturity as we use our judgment, make decisions, take initiative and work with God to honour him and grow in our relationship with him.

3. God rewards us

But just because God may feel distant and he has given us freedom does not mean that what we do with what we have been given doesn't matter to God. In some ways the accounting scene at the end of this parable reminds me of the boardroom moment in the TV programme *The Apprentice*. Boss Sir Alan Sugar asks the individuals what they have contributed to the task he has set, and the one who has contributed the least is fired, while those who have contributed most are rewarded. Jesus will never fire us or forsake us, but he wants us to know that there is an expectation that we will invest our talents for the benefit of God's kingdom, and he warns us not to waste them out of fear, laziness or thoughtlessness.

In the next seven days, we will begin to take stock of the 'talents' God has given us, so we can begin to work out how we can best invest them for God. But reminding ourselves right at the beginning that we work for God will help us throughout our lives. For those of us who will be self-employed or destined to reach the top of our fields, it is helpful to remember that we are still under the authority of God. For those of us who will struggle with immoral or incompetent bosses, we will be well prepared to know that we are first and foremost accountable to God. For those of us who find ourselves unemployed with time on our hands, it is reassuring to know that in God's world there is a zero unemployment rate – he still has work for us to do.

What can you learn from this parable about being managed/ managing people? What would you look for in an employer/ employee? Think of some ways you can invest your talents today for God's kingdom. Here are some ideas, or think of your own:

'I will invest an hour of my time today in helping somebody.'

'I will invest a day's spending money in an organization working in the Two-Thirds World.'

'I will invest my access to the web by posting my testimony on the internet.'

 Further study: Read Luke 6:27–38. What practical tips can you gain from this passage about how God expects you to invest your talents?

 Prayer: Thank God for the responsibilities, resources, respect and rewards he gives you as your master. Meditate on God's words: 'Well done, good and faithful servant. Come and share your master's happiness.'

In the early part of my career, I was quite a tyrannical boss. What I've learnt over the years is that if you invest in people and demonstrate clearly that you want the best for them and from them, then the vast majority of folk respect that and will work hard as a result. This has the double benefit of being good for whatever business you're in, and being what Christ would have us do. Justin

'Your kingdom come . . . on earth as it is in heaven'

Reflecting on the past week's studies, try to fill in this table to help you summarize or decide your lifelong Christian principles as you face the future:

	Principles in my faith	Principles in my work
CAREER		
AMBITIONS		
QUALIFICATIONS		
JOB SECURITY		
WORKPLACE		
REWARD		
BOSS		

week 2

Identifying your vocation

Monday:
Mandate

Tuesday:
Passions

Wednesday:
Gifts

Thursday:
Needs

Friday:
Experiences

Saturday:
Opportunities

Sunday:
Destiny

> Then God said, 'Let us make human beings in our image, in our likeness, so that they may rule over the fish in the sea and the birds in the sky, over the livestock and all the wild animals, and over all the creatures that move along the ground.'
>
> So God created human beings
>   in his own image,
>   in the image of God he created them;
>   male and female
>   he created them.
>
> God blessed them and said to them, 'Be fruitful and increase in number; fill the earth and subdue it. Rule over the fish in the sea and the birds in the sky and over every living creature that moves on the ground.'
> (Genesis 1:26–28)

Sleeping rough in a snow-covered Parisian park, the amnesiac wakes up from his bench bed to find two security guards towering over him. As they begin their assault, instinct kicks in, and before he knows it, he has taken out the guards with his bare hands. As he looks at the pair strewn in the snow, Jason Bourne looks at his hands with a host of questions on his mind. Who am I? What is my line of work? Am I a good guy or a bad guy?

Identity, vocation and self-image are inextricably linked. 'What do you do?' is predictably the second question we ask when we meet someone for the first time. And when job direction or security become uncertain, many people feel like they don't know who they are any more. What we intrinsically long for is a clear mandate to know what we are supposed to be doing with our lives. This passage in Genesis has to be the first stop in any investigation into our vocation. It demonstrates to us that mankind and mandate go together as we see God's invention of human life and his intention for our life direction. We can learn three vital starting points as to what God wants us to do with our lives from this passage.

1. Value

We are all made in God's image, irrespective of age, gender, intellect, looks, sexual orientation, abilities, disabilities, skin colour, social standing or popularity. This makes us intrinsically valuable, and worthy of respect, love and compassion. Even after the fall of humankind God still says we are made in his image (Genesis 9:6), and despite the fact that each of us is damaged, rebellious and selfish, God still chooses to have us bear his image to the world. The privilege of being made in God's image gives us a mandate to honour him in the way we treat one another.

2. Visibility

My adopted daughter does not share a biological connection with me, although a surprising number of people point out physical resemblances. But her behaviour, accent, and mannerisms definitely resemble those of my other children. Similarly our identity as God's children and image-bearers has to do with how we act rather than with how we look. Our mandate is to make God our Father visible by displaying his character to a watching world, taking our lead from the example of Jesus, the ultimate 'image-bearer'.

3. Vocation

As soon as God created the first people, he gave them a mandate to occupy the earth and to be occupied with the earth. Work was introduced before the fall as a fundamental and significant part of our identity, encompassing three universal elements. Firstly, we are to pursue a relationship with God to fulfil our call as image-bearer. Secondly, we are to pursue harmonious relationship with others. Being called by God was not a private experience, but a communal challenge as men and women were to work together to mirror God, and to multiply and fill the earth. Thirdly, we are to pursue a relationship with the earth, as we are told to take care of God's creation and rule responsibly over it.

Any job we consider should incorporate these three elements as part of our mandate. Or, put negatively, any job that would involve the breaking of relationship with God, people or creation should be avoided. Unfortunately the world of work is not so clear-cut. I once heard a compelling argument suggesting that Christians should not work for a crisp manufacturer – the speaker believed that turning a healthy potato into an unhealthy crisp involved sabotaging creation as well as sabotaging the welfare of the general public. Since I love salty snacks, I find it difficult to agree, but the point is that we need to be clear in our minds and in our consciences of our mandate, and look for work that fits into that vocation.

In our world, many people suffer from insecurity, low self-esteem, and lack of purpose and identity. Often these problems can become exacerbated in the workplace when we are overloaded or overlooked. But what God has for us is an overriding mandate that gives us value, visibility and a vocation, whatever career we choose, and whatever goes on around us in the workplace.

Whatever our career choice, we have three vital aspects of our vocation. Fill in the chart below to see how that might look within different professions or within your profession options.

	Working on my relationship with God	Working on my relationship with others	Working on my relationship with the planet
Teacher			
Engineer			
Artist			
Other			

 Further study: Read through Genesis 1 – 3: How do the fall and the curse make all of these universal vocations more complicated?

 Prayer: Prayerfully consider what action you could take today as a student to pursue your mandate.

Coming to the end of my third year, I was very worried about not having a clear direction for the future. On one particular day the Lord spoke to me so clearly from Proverbs 4:18. He told me that as Christians we shouldn't expect to have plans A–Z of our lives figured out (as the world expects you to), but rather, as we trust him and depend on him, he will make our path shine brighter and brighter . . . like the sun! Alex

> And now, brothers and sisters, we want you to know about the grace that God has given the Macedonian churches. In the midst of a very severe trial, their overflowing joy and their extreme poverty welled up in rich generosity. For I testify that they gave as much as they were able, and even beyond their ability. Entirely on their own, they urgently pleaded with us for the privilege of sharing in this service to the Lord's people. And they went beyond our expectations; having given themselves first of all to the Lord, they gave themselves by the will of God also to us . . . But since you excel in everything – in faith, in speech, in knowledge, in complete earnestness and in the love we have kindled in you – see that you also excel in this grace of giving.
>
> I am not commanding you, but I want to test the sincerity of your love by comparing it with the earnestness of others. For you know the grace of our Lord Jesus Christ, that though he was rich, yet for your sake he became poor, so that you through his poverty might become rich.
>
> (2 Corinthians 8:1–9)

It is no secret that I hated my chemistry degree with a passion. The laborious labs, followed by report writing, were in my mind the very epitome of meaningless monotony. The only thing that kept me going was the idea that perhaps one day I would discover a brand new renewable energy source or the cure for cancer. But by my final year I finally had to come to terms with the fact that this was not what was going to happen on a university campus near me. My love of volleyball had also faded during my university years, but what I discovered growing in me was a passion for evangelism, books and travel. The problem was that with all the talk about qualifications and CVs, nobody was interested in the things that really fired me up.

But the Bible is not so dismissive of passions. It recognizes that some of our cravings can lead us far away from God and into a lot of trouble. But it also recognizes that some of our desires are God-given, and can lead us into effective service. The apostle Paul strikes me as a passionate man – passionate about the gospel, and about the church, even about letter writing. And in this paragraph of his letter to the Corinthian church he gives us an example of a godly passion that he spotted in the church in Macedonia.

1. Passion is both caught and taught

Some people may say at this point that they have no passions, or that they are not passionate people. But this passage shows us that passion can be either a divine gift or a divine charge. Although the Macedonians received their generous spirit from God, the Corinthians were encouraged to adopt it in their own lives. Sometimes we feel a spontaneous passion for something; at other times it is through a friend or the media that we are provoked to action. I was challenged recently by a nine-year-old boy who heard about orphans in Africa who had to walk sixteen miles to school. He asked God what he could do and started a sponsored basketball throw-a-thon. After three years he raised enough money to build a school in Zambia and is now working on raising funds for a health centre. The infectious enthusiasm of this lad obviously impassioned others to give generously.

2. Passion is both ordinary and extraordinary

The passion in the hearts of the Macedonian Christians was nothing unusual. They simply cared about others. But their simple act of charity became an extraordinary passion for them. Even though they were under persecution and on the poverty line themselves, they gave beyond what was expected and even beyond their means. They wanted to give, begged to give, and enjoyed every penny they put in the collection – nothing was going to stop them. I love to see people fired up in this way. An ordinary passion to teach children can make for the most extraordinary teachers. An ordinary passion for efficiency can transform an office or an organization. An ordinary passion for friendships can revolutionize any communal environment into an extraordinary experience of acceptance and love.

3. Passion is both grace-fuelled and grace-filled

Paul makes the connection in this passage between the generosity of the Macedonians and the grace of Jesus. Jesus set the example and the standard of costly sacrifice for the sake of others. Giving generously and without expectation of reciprocity is characteristic of passion. If you believe God has given you a passion for playing a musical instrument, then it is natural to want to play that instrument to bring pleasure to God and to others. A passion for computer programming can similarly be used generously in worship to God for his glory, as well as for the benefit of a company.

Eric Liddell had two great passions in life. He felt a call to be a missionary in China. He was also an athlete with ambition. What was remarkable about Liddell was that he did not see these passions as mutually exclusive. Liddell raced to gain a gold medal and a world record at the Olympic Games. He also went on to become a cross-cultural missionary, eventually dying in China in a prisoner-of-war camp run by the Japanese army. Some well-meaning church leader may have advised him as a student that his missionary calling would be more eternally significant than his athletic calling. But Liddell rightly saw the opportunity to honour God through both of his passions, as he famously said: 'God made me for China, but he also made me fast. When I run, I feel his pleasure.'

 When were your happiest and most fulfilled moments as a child, teenager and student? Make a list and try to deduce from them what your passions are, or what passions are beginning to develop. Make a list of career options where they could be used.

 Further study: Psalm 37:4 says: 'Take delight in the LORD, and he will give you the desires of your heart.' Rather than seeing this verse as a blank cheque from God to do whatever we want, read through the whole of this psalm and write down some checks to make sure that our passions are pleasing and honouring to God.

 Prayer: What do you enjoy doing that also enables you to feel God's pleasure? Adapt 2 Thessalonians 1:11–12 into a prayer to God about your passions.

On finishing university I had no clue what to do . . . and so I became a school dinner lady for a few months! It was a really hard time as I didn't want to use my degree directly. I was fed up with studying, and I didn't want to serve lasagne and chips for the rest of my life. During this time God humbled me and opened a door into 'missions' that I really didn't want to take. It meant moving home for a while and a rubbish wage, but with hindsight, I am so glad I listened to God, as this open door enabled me to grow in confidence, to discern my passions and to be mentored.
Andy

> Just as a body, though one, has many parts, but all its many parts form one body, so it is with Christ. For we were all baptised by one Spirit so as to form one body – whether Jews or Gentiles, slave or free – and we were all given the one Spirit to drink. And so the body is not made up of one part but of many.
>
> Now if the foot should say, 'Because I am not a hand, I do not belong to the body,' it would not for that reason cease to be part of the body. And if the ear should say, 'Because I am not an eye, I do not belong to the body,' it would not for that reason cease to be part of the body. If the whole body were an eye, where would the sense of hearing be? If the whole body were an ear, where would the sense of smell be? But in fact God has placed the parts in the body, every one of them, just as he wanted them to be. If they were all one part, where would the body be? As it is, there are many parts, but one body.
>
> (1 Corinthians 12:12–20)

I never know whether to laugh or cry at talent shows. Some acts look promising but are truly painful to watch, and then there are other acts that look fated from the beginning but turn out to be utterly sensational. Seeing the bizarre, the bendy and the brilliant side by side perfectly illustrates that we are all truly unique. It is this diversity in human life that Paul celebrates when he talks about the church as a body made up of different parts. There is no way we could judge whether the melodic vocal chord or the methodical heart valves get the X factor, or whether there is more talent in the sensitivity of a taste bud or the flexibility of a finger. Paul makes the point that it is no use wishing to be something else when we were created to perform a unique function.

We have already seen that God has given us a common mandate, but also a variety of passions. Today we will see how the Spirit gives each of us a different set of gifts. We cannot put an order in for the ones we fancy or add them to a spiritual wish-list; these are the sort of gifts that we discover, receive or unwrap, and Paul points out four criteria.

1. Designed by God

Did you hear about the woman who told her husband she didn't mind what he got her for Christmas, so long as it contained diamonds? He told her he didn't mind what she got for him so long as it went from 0–200 in less than ten seconds. I would have loved to have been there at that 'priceless' moment on Christmas morning when the wife opened a packet of playing cards, and her husband opened a set of bathroom scales! Sometimes we can feel short-changed by our spiritual gifts, because we fancy the extravagant, exciting ones. (There have been many times whilst hosting a small group that I would gladly have swapped the gift of hospitality for the gift of healing!) But whatever gifts God has for us, we can be confident that he has not been cheap like the couple in the story. We have not earned our gift, we do not deserve it, and in fact what we have is something perfect for us and priceless, with the designer's label all over it.

2. Dispensed through the Spirit

Paul tells us clearly that every believer is given the same Spirit and so, regardless of ethnic background, gender or social status, we are all made part of the body of Christ with no room for division. Ironically these things that unite us often make Christians fall out – about the role of the Spirit in the church, about how we worship God, or about the different views of the roles of men and women. But if the Spirit is at work in us he will draw us together in interdependence, just like the parts of the body that Paul uses in his analogy.

3. Displayed by the church

There is a predictable moment in most superhero movies from the *Fantastic Four* to *The Watchmen* or *The Incredibles*, when the superheroes work out that their gifts are better used in combination than in isolation. And so it is with spiritual gifts – the whole is greater than the sum of its parts in the church. Paul's illustration of the human body fits perfectly as the ultimate symbiotic relationship. Yet often in the church – and here in Corinth this is exactly the problem – we live as if our gifts are given to us as something to be framed and hung over the mantelpiece to be occasionally enjoyed by us and admired by others. But spiritual gifts are as inappropriate as body parts for such treatment. Our gifts should be displayed in the church where they can be nurtured without nursing the ego; exercised without becoming exaggerated; cultivated yet controlled. This does not mean that all Christians should seek a career in the church – but the church is a 24/7 community and commitment, even when we are scattered in different workplaces. This does not mean that we should expect to walk into a church and our gifts be immediately maximized – any organ transplant may take a while to be accepted by the body, and in the meantime we may need to seek to serve primarily where the needs are.

4. Discovered by you?

We have seen that our spiritual gifts are not earned or acquired through our own effort, but are divinely and graciously awakened and enabled in us by the Holy Spirit for the building of the church. Discovering our gifts cannot therefore be done in isolation, but in consultation with our Christian family. We are responsible for discovering our own gifts, but being part of a local church and a Christian Union can help others to recognize and develop gifts in us, whether they are gifts of sense (e.g. discernment, knowledge), of state (e.g. celibacy, poverty), of speaking (e.g. preaching, prophecy), or of service (e.g. mercy, hospitality). There are four chapters of the New Testament given to this as a lesson for the early church, and so as young Christians we too should set aside serious time to consider what God has gifted us with, and whether this will impact our career choice.

 Look through the lists of gifts with your church leader and identify the ones you believe God is developing in you: 1 Corinthians 12, Romans 12, Ephesians 4, and 1 Peter 4.

 Further study: Take a look at the call of Moses (Exodus 3 – 4). What can we learn about the connections between our perceptions of our gifting, our openness to God's call and his ultimate plan?

 Prayer: After reluctantly following God's call on his life, Moses learns to appreciate God's choice of gifts. Meditate on and echo his prayer in Psalm 90:17: 'May the favour of the Lord our God rest on us; establish the work of our hands for us – yes, establish the work of our hands.'

I didn't really know what I wanted to do when I graduated, so I spent quite a lot of time in prayer asking for guidance. I never heard a booming voice or anything like that, but over time I realized what my major gifts were and where I thought God wanted me to go, and ultimately the right option made itself apparent. I checked this with lots of friends and they all said it was perfect for me, so I went ahead and haven't looked back! AJ

> Do nothing out of selfish ambition or vain conceit. Rather, in humility value others above yourselves, not looking to your own interests but each of you to the interests of the others.
>
> In your relationships with one another, have the same attitude of mind Christ Jesus had:
>
> who, being in very nature God,
>> did not consider equality with God something to be used to his own advantage;
>
> rather, he made himself nothing
>> by taking the very nature of a servant,
>> being made in human likeness.
>
> And being found in appearance as a human being,
>> he humbled himself
>> by becoming obedient to death – even death on a cross!
>
> (Philippians 2:3–8)

The 200,000 tonne cargo ship was being tossed about like a rubber dinghy, and waves like skyscrapers were doing their utmost to sink it. The crew on board couldn't remember such a terrible storm and were preparing for the worst. In the distance a helicopter was battling with the gale-force winds but, as it came closer, one of its occupants launched himself out of the open door and into mid-air with nothing but what looked like a tiny spider web thread. As I tucked into my crisps and hot chocolate from the comfort of my cosy sofa, he lowered himself carefully onto the ship to rescue the sailors. *World's Most Scary Rescues 4* made great TV, but in fact the man who had left his sofa and hot chocolate to enter the danger zone was no actor. He probably could have had a career in Hollywood as a stuntman if he had chosen to. Equally he could have pursued a career as an Olympic swimmer.

Both would have probably paid better and offered him a longer life expectancy. But his chosen profession was to use his dedication and agility to save other people's lives, putting his own in constant danger.

When Jesus chose to descend to earth, he left behind all the comforts of paradise to live with discomfort and danger. Here in Philippians 2 we are given a description of his downward mobility. Beginning with the privileges of being God in heaven, he chose to leave behind his illustrious position and be born as a baby into the most ignominious of circumstances. But as if that wasn't enough, he downgraded from being someone with potential for power to being a man prepared to serve the needs of others. Then he selflessly gave up even his last human right to live and accepted the death penalty, not for his own crimes, but for the selfishness of others. Jesus' unique humility and servanthood are laid out for us as a pattern for the normal Christian life. As we look for advice and help regarding our own ambitions and future, we are told to look at Christ's selfless example.

1. Looking to learn

Often we fail even to see other people's struggles because we are distracted by events in our own lives. But looking out for others needs to be more than a cursory glance at the headlines or muttering a predictable 'how are you?' to those we meet. It means first of all that we learn to open our eyes to the needs of the world and the people around us.

2. Looking to love

Secondly, being told to look not only to our own interests but also to the interests of others implies that there will sometimes be a difference or even conflict of interests and then we have a choice. The Good Samaritan illustrates this well: the man chose to delay his own journey, put aside his prejudices and give away his supplies for the sake of a total stranger.

3. Looking to lose

'The problem with the rat race is that even if you win, you're still a rat,' quipped the American comedienne, Lily Tomlin. She has a point. Our calling to be Christlike means going against the flow. This may well mean not seeking to be upwardly mobile just to get riches for ourselves, but following Jesus' downward mobility to reach out to the poor and needy.

Katy avoids her former head teacher. Her private school instilled in her ambitions for Oxbridge and beyond, but her passion and gifting were not in Classics or sciences but in art. Perhaps the head teacher could have been won over if Katy were exhibiting in exclusive European galleries. But Katy is teaching art in a failing school in an urban priority area. She gets no mention in Old Girls' newsletters and hasn't been invited to speak at the annual prize-giving or present the awards on sports day. But although she has won no glory for her school, she brings Jesus glory each day because she is a faithful servant looking to the needs of others.

C. T. Studd studied at Cambridge and became a world-class cricketer. But despite these extraordinary athletic and academic gifts, God called him to put the needs of others first and become a cross-cultural missionary in China. He described his passion like this: 'Some wish to live within the sound of a chapel bell; I wish to run a rescue mission within a yard of hell.'

Like Katy, some Christians may be called to use their careers not to win the rat-race, but to trail behind for the benefit of others. Other Christians, such as C. T. Studd, may be called to set aside their natural career paths in order to seek and save the lost. As we consider our own gifts, opportunities, experiences and options, the challenge is also to consider the needs of those around us and allow that to influence our choices.

 Think about the needs of those around you: physical, emotional, spiritual and practical. What can you do about these needs today and during the course of your career?

 Further study: Look at the following Bible characters: Daniel, Esther, Moses and Joseph. In what ways were they prepared to be upwardly and downwardly mobile for the sake of others? In what ways did God elevate them for his glory?

 Prayer: Imagine the people around you bowing to Jesus and confessing him as Lord. Pray that this image would inspire you and motivate you to consider their needs above your own today and in your career choices.

I trained as an opera singer and was working in the music industry, when one day I became aware of the plight of trafficked people. I couldn't ignore the problem and so made it the focus of my life to mobilize the church to bring an end to this evil trade. I put on an awareness event at the NEC arena and founded an anti-trafficking organization called Hope for Justice. I still work as a vocal coach, which gives me an opportunity to honour God with my musical gifts, and also helps pay for my work among the world's poor. Ben

> Hear, O Israel: The LORD our God, the LORD is one. Love the LORD your God with all your heart and with all your soul and with all your strength. These commandments that I give you today are to be on your hearts. Impress them on your children. Talk about them when you sit at home and when you walk along the road, when you lie down and when you get up. Tie them as symbols on your hands and bind them on your foreheads. Write them on the doorframes of your houses and on your gates.
>
> When the LORD your God brings you into the land he swore to your fathers, to Abraham, Isaac and Jacob, to give you – a land with large, flourishing cities you did not build, houses filled with all kinds of good things you did not provide, wells you did not dig, and vineyards and olive groves you did not plant – then when you eat and are satisfied, be careful that you do not forget the LORD, who brought you out of Egypt, out of the land of slavery.
>
> Fear the LORD your God, serve him only and take your oaths in his name.
>
> (Deuteronomy 6:4–13)

An old man dressed in a suit was found wandering around the centre of town. He was in a state of some distress, and after a while a kind woman asked him what was wrong. He said, 'I am a very rich man and I have just got married to a beautiful young woman, who seems to love me for who I am, not just for my fabulous wealth. We are about to enjoy a passion-filled honeymoon together and she is waiting at home for me right now.' The woman couldn't understand why this would make him so distressed. On asking him, the old man turned to her and said, 'I don't remember where I live.'

Memory is vital, especially when we are away from home or on a journey, and remembering where we have come from will have a huge impact on where we are going. Some of us are unable to venture into the future because of the baggage of our past. Others of us would love to forget about the past and hope that passing our finals would afford us a clean break. But God has a habit of helping us to deal with our past and move on. The idea of looking backwards to find out where God might be taking us is a thoroughly biblical concept. David's slingshot training against wolves and lions as he protected his sheep enabled him to single-handedly defeat the enemy of God's people. Mary's alabaster jar of perfume, probably bought with the profits of her prostitution, was symbolically poured out in generous devotion and worship. Onesimus's escape from slavery led to his conversion, and then to a restored and repaired relationship with his owner. Past and future experiences are tied together in God's plans.

In this passage God has to remind people of their past. Some would forget because of the comforts they would experience as they entered the Promised Land. Some would forget because they would be tempted to follow the crowd. Some would forget because it was easier to be the master of their own lives. Some would forget because their families would not pass on the values or the stories they had learned. God's warnings of forgetfulness were to come true over and over again, and the Old Testament story follows the cycle of forgetting God, getting into trouble and remembering to call on his help again and again.

This cycle of forgetting and remembering God is just as prevalent today. Many Christians leave university and get drawn away from their faith by the comforts, the crowds, and the confusions of life and family. Often they get drawn back to faith when there is trouble. As the story of Israel demonstrates, God is gracious to receive us back when we let him down in this way. But perhaps we can avoid the pain by basing our lives on three unforgettable things:

1. God's unchanging character

This passage challenges us to make sure that God is central to our lives, not just when calamity strikes, but all the time. He is the God through the crisis of the exodus, but also through the settled life in the Promised Land. God's character does not change, but our memory and experience of him do, so we would do well to allow every aspect of our life to be infiltrated by our faith.

2. God's unchanging commands

God asks us to weave his words into our hearts and into our daily lives. Reflecting on Scripture is to be part of our normal routine, part of our family life, part of our public life. It is to be breathed in like the oxygen vital for life. It is to be talked about, thought about, lived and loved to remind us constantly of why we do what we do, and to protect us from harm.

3. God's unchanging commitment

God's commitment had brought the people out of slavery despite their grumbling and their greed for other gods. But even when they were to arrive in the Promised Land with all its blessings, the danger was that they would look back at the past and remember the problems. But God did not want them to remember the hunger pangs, the venomous snakes and the bloody battles, but rather the miraculous manna, supernatural victories and his clear guidance.

Many students choose a career because of experiences in their own lives. Negative experiences can bring about positive influence, just as the people of Israel were called to be generous to those they employed because of their experience of slavery (Deuteronomy 10). Somebody who has had a positive or negative experience of the care system may be inspired to go on to a career in social work to help others. Someone who has nursed a parent may go on to a career in medicine. These experiences mould us, often even define us, and are legitimate factors in the way we go about choosing a career.

 What experiences in your past stand out? How can you see God's guidance already in your life? Are there things in your past you need to repent of, learn from, be continually reminded of, move on from, or deal with? How could they be used for God's glory?

 Further study: Read Paul's letter to Philemon and consider the different jobs Onesimus had. How did God reconcile Onesimus's past, present and future? What can we learn from this?

 Prayer: Ask God to help you remember times in your life when he has used you, spoken to you and led you. Ask for God's help in integrating his eternal word into your everyday life.

I enjoyed welcoming international students at Warwick uni. I asked around about where I could carry on doing the same kind of stuff and pass on what I'd learnt. I applied and was accepted to be a UCCF Relay Worker.
Judith

> Now I want you to know, brothers and sisters, that what has happened to me has actually served to advance the gospel. As a result, it has become clear throughout the whole palace guard and to everyone else that I am in chains for Christ. And because of my chains, most of the brothers and sisters have become confident in the Lord and dare all the more to proclaim the gospel without fear.
>
> It is true that some preach Christ out of envy and rivalry, but others out of goodwill. The latter do so out of love, knowing that I am put here for the defence of the gospel. The former preach Christ out of selfish ambition, not sincerely, supposing that they can stir up trouble for me while I am in chains. But what does it matter? The important thing is that in every way, whether from false motives or true, Christ is preached. And because of this I rejoice.
> (Philippians 1:12–18)

There's a story flying round the internet involving four people named Everybody, Somebody, Anybody and Nobody. There was an important job to be done and Everybody was asked to do it. Anybody could have done it, but Nobody did it. Somebody got angry about that, because it was Everybody's job. Everybody thought Anybody could do it, but Nobody realized that Everybody wouldn't do it. Consequently, it ended up that Nobody told Anybody, so Everybody blamed Somebody.

The story makes me think of a hundred different scenarios that I have been involved in. In every office, family, church and club around the world, there seems to be a constant battle of delegating, complaining, shirking and blaming. Maybe you have seen it in your church or work experience. But this way of thinking can also infect our way of living and influence how we decide about our future life direction. Philippians offers us a healthy antidote. Instead of looking for opportunities to avoid responsibility and blame others when it all goes pear-shaped, we see a radically different attitude – a willingness to take responsibility for those around us and to live opportunistically for the gospel.

Opportunities come in surprising places

If anyone had a reason to complain it was Paul. His vocation was to travel and preach, and yet here he was under house arrest, chained to a corner of a room with only his captors for company. Had I been in his shoes I would have been demanding a meeting with my lawyers, and letting everyone know that I was a victim of injustice. Or I would have been seething as I contemplated all the opportunities I was missing out on because of my imprisonment. But Paul did not see this sudden change in circumstance as invalidating his calling. Instead, beginning with the guy holding a sword across his doorway, he shared the good news of Jesus. Each time there was a changing of the guard, Paul would begin again, and soon the whole palace security attaché had heard the gospel. Living opportunistically like this allows us to live powerfully for God wherever we find ourselves, even when life doesn't work out the way we expected.

Opportunities come in surprising people

Paul's status in the early church obviously drew out some jealous rivals, and so when Paul was imprisoned, they saw an opportunity too good to miss. Jostling into position to fill Paul's shoes in his absence, word got back to him of the apparent backstabbing. Again, Paul had every right to be livid, to reassert his authority and to dismiss the wannabes. But again, Paul had at the forefront of his mind the opportunities this afforded for the gospel, and he rejoiced that the whole mess had resulted in a mass of preachers.

Many finalists considering future career options are swayed enormously by the opportunities that crop up. A supportive tutor who opens the door to a Master's programme, a successful interview, or a sudden inheritance can make us feel we should jump into further study, a particular job or a year of travelling. But we see from this passage that we should make a few checks.

Firstly, is our glass half-full of opportunities, or half-empty? Paul did not dwell on the opportunities he could have been taking up, but focused on the situation right under his nose despite the circumstances. Secondly, is our opportunism based on gospel or greed? Paul was prepared to take risks because of his desire to see people engage with the gospel, but some of his rivals were motivated purely by status and respect. Thirdly, are we prepared to check that an opportunity is right for us? We see from this passage that when the vacancy came up of 'itinerant church-planter', many people leapt into this role, some of whom were not suited for it. Fourthly, is our opportunism gracious or grabby? When confronted with the betrayal of his colleagues, Paul could have ruined their career plans, and yet he decided not to judge but to be gracious.

I once got to know a Russian prisoner, who had been placed in solitary confinement for trying to convert his cellmates during Communism. All Alexander had was a bed and a hole in the ground connected to the sewer. Yet from this room Alexander changed eternity. He discovered the sewers were interconnected, so by sticking his head down the hole and shouting, he could communicate to the prisoner in the next cell. Despite the stench, he led his neighbour to faith in Christ. His faith was as irrepressible as his passion was contagious, and his story continues to inspire me.

 What are the opportunities available to you after university? Think about your motivations under these headings. Is there any overlap?

- Good for the gospel
- Good for the kingdom
- Good for me
- Good for others

 Further study: Print out 2 Kings 5. Jot in the margins the jobs of the people involved in the story. Highlight in green all the opportunities taken that were good, and highlight the missed opportunities in red. What can we learn from this?

 Prayer: Ask God to give you three gospel opportunities today. Enjoy discovering them. Consider making this a habit.

I wanted to work in Poland after university, but I was told there were no opportunities. When I went to a prayer meeting for Belarus, a headline came up that IFES needed men for their team that year. I glanced up to see my best friend looking at me with a very meaningful look on her face. To cut a long story short, I ended up spending two amazing years in Belarus. Matthew

But whatever were gains to me I now consider loss for the sake of Christ. What is more, I consider everything a loss compared to the surpassing worth of knowing Christ Jesus my Lord, for whose sake I have lost all things. I consider them garbage, that I may gain Christ and be found in him, not having a righteousness of my own that comes from the law, but that which is through faith in Christ – the righteousness that comes from God on the basis of faith. I want to know Christ – yes, to know the power of his resurrection and participation in his sufferings, becoming like him in his death, and so, somehow, attaining to the resurrection from the dead.

Not that I have already obtained all this, or have already arrived at my goal, but I press on to take hold of that for which Christ Jesus took hold of me. Brothers and sisters, I do not consider myself yet to have taken hold of it. But one thing I do: forgetting what is behind and straining towards what is ahead, I press on towards the goal to win the prize for which God has called me heavenwards in Christ Jesus.

(Philippians 3:7–14)

It was the school 4 by 100-metre relay race. I was going to be running the glory leg – the champion taking the final bend, bringing the baton home, and crossing the line first to the roar of the crowd. At least that was the plan. I stood there in lane five straining forward, no turning back, waiting to hear the footsteps of my teammate. I wanted the prize so badly and I was about to give it everything I had – until my teammate went sailing past me in lane four, muttering something unrepeatable under his breath. Disappointed and disqualified I learned my lesson. I had strained toward what was ahead, but hadn't taken stock of what was behind.

When Paul took stock of what was behind him – his family status, his high-flying education, his position in society and accolades he had won – he summed it up as excrement. He knew that focusing on them would only distract him in his Christian life. What he chose to hold on to instead was the cross and the resurrection that would motivate him to achieve his destiny. But he is surely not saying that we may as well flush our textbooks down the toilet or incinerate our course work. So how do our degree, our vocation and our destiny all fit together?

1. A destiny that energizes not exhausts

By the time Paul was writing his letter to the Philippians, he had already had an incredibly exciting and fruitful time as a follower of Jesus. He had seen many people converted, he had authored letters that would later be included into the canon of Scripture, he had defended the faith, faced persecution, planted churches and discipled leaders. Paul could easily have felt that the pressure was off. Instead, he reiterated that he was not bowing out gracefully, but sprinting his way to the finish line. If we have worked hard and served God faithfully at university, we might feel we are ready to change down a gear, or that we deserve some slack, but Paul encourages us to keep striving in anticipation of the exciting things God still has to do in our lives.

2. A destiny of maturity not mediocrity

Despite all his achievements, his face-to-face encounter with the risen Christ, and his incredible impact on the growth of Christianity globally, Paul still believes he has a way to go in his spiritual maturity. Many Christians I know would consider themselves 'mature' in the faith after just a few years, and we tend to compare ourselves to those around us. But Paul encourages us to compare ourselves to the perfection of Jesus and reminds us to keep going.

3. A destiny of the immortal, not the immediate

When we are used to downing Red Bull in order to stay awake long enough to get the assignment in by 9 am, or when we are used to the panic of waking up just ten minutes before the lecture begins, we begin to feel that our destiny is simply to get over the hurdles of the never-ending deadlines. But Paul is not motivated reluctantly by the rush of the immediate, but gladly by the promise of the immortal. Our destiny involves discarding the stuff that hinders us, reaching for the imperishable, and transforming the mundane into the magnificent on the path that Jesus has set for us.

Paul's vocation was as a preacher and apostle. He was destined to become the most influential figure in the church through his written work. We may not know our destiny, but we will discover it eventually if we fulfil our God-given vocation right to the end. This week we have looked at our mandate, our gifts, our passions, our experiences, our opportunities and the needs around us. It is where these things converge that we will find our vocation. But while we are taking stock of this, Paul challenges us to keep it all in perspective with a reminder of our ultimate destiny: 'But whatever were gains to me I now consider loss . . . because of the surpassing worth of knowing Christ Jesus my Lord.'

 Draw a graph of your spiritual life marking growth against time. Project that line into the future. Will the gradient become steeper, or do you expect to plateau, or even fall away? Mark on long-term goals you have for any area of your life.

Further study: Samson (Judges 16), Saul (1 Samuel 13) and Solomon (1 Kings 11) are three examples of men who gave up too early and missed their destiny – find out why.

 Prayer:
Father God. Thank you that you have taken hold of me for a purpose. My destiny. To burn. To grow. To win. To sprint to the finish. To endure. To enjoy. To be energized. To become like you. To be with you. Help me choose a path that will enable me to reach my potential and realize your glory. My destiny. Amen

As a student doing speech therapy, I had two wishes. In my final year, I became aware of a group of physiotherapists who were looking for a speech therapist to join their venture. I approached them and straightaway was invited to start after my graduation. But I needed a part-time job to give me a basic income so that I could develop my practice from scratch. I was accepted in a hospital as an audiologist, which gave me a secure income. One year later, my practice had become established – one dream fulfilled. And then, as a gift, I was invited by the university to become a part-time lecturer. My second dream came true. God had heard my prayer, seen my initiatives and had in his time given me what I desired to do with my degree. Marijke

'Your kingdom come . . . on earth as it is in heaven'

Reflecting on the past week's inspirations, fill in this diagram to help you identify your vocation:

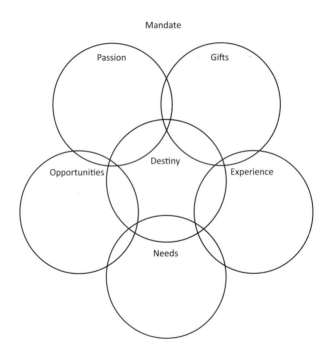

Mandate

Passion

Gifts

Destiny

Opportunities

Experience

Needs

week 3

Navigating your route

Monday:
The backpacker

Tuesday:
The Masters

Wednesday:
The fresh start

Thursday:
The jobseeker

Friday:
The volunteer

Saturday:
The missionary

Sunday:
The wedding planner

> Where can I go from your Spirit?
>   Where can I flee from your presence?
> If I go up to the heavens, you are there;
>   if I make my bed in the depths, you are there.
> If I rise on the wings of the dawn,
>   if I settle on the far side of the sea,
> even there your hand will guide me,
>   your right hand will hold me fast.
> If I say, 'Surely the darkness will hide me
>   and the light become night around me,'
> even the darkness will not be dark to you;
>   the night will shine like the day,
>   for darkness is as light to you.
> For you created my inmost being;
>   you knit me together in my mother's womb.
> I praise you because I am fearfully and wonderfully made;
>   your works are wonderful,
>   I know that full well.
> (Psalm 139:7–14)

One day I was looking out of the window of a friend's house in British Columbia, Canada, and I saw the blow spouts of whales. A phenomenon this close to the shoreline occurs only once in ten years, and I had the privilege of being in the right place at the right time. My travels for work have certainly brought me some of the most memorable occasions in my life. I was in Chicago the day Barack Obama was elected President of the USA. I have eaten caviar in Russia and my grandmother's homemade curry in Malaysia. I have broken into a youth hostel in the Slovakian mountains and been thrown off a tram in Hungary. I have been shot at in two separate countries. I have encountered a wild bear in the grounds of a hotel in Colorado. I have flown over Albania in a six-seater plane and I have crossed the Black Sea in a fisherman's ferry. The world God created is absolutely amazing, and I have experienced only the tiniest fraction of it. It is no wonder that many of us feel the urge to see as much as we can for ourselves, and the period between 'education' and 'career' is one of the prime opportunities. But for those of us considering this option, and asking if it is the right thing to do, are there any biblical principles we can apply?

God's fingerprints

Our great Creator God made us to explore and enjoy his world. In the opening chapters of Genesis we are given a panoramic picture of creation and we are told all of it is good – from the diversity of the animal world, to the buried gold in the land of Havillah and the fine detail of the flora and fauna. The cultural mandate given to humanity, which involved exploring, cultivating and enjoying God's creation, has never been revoked and is written into the job description of being human. Travel will expose our senses and imaginations to more of God's glory displayed in creation, and inspire and fuel us to praise God.

God's presence

God is continually encouraging people to get out more – from Abraham to Paul, from Jonah to Nehemiah. God asks people to leave the security of their surroundings and to trust him by serving his purposes in the world. So when Abraham leaves his family, God promises his blessing and a new family. When the people of Israel are called to leave Egypt, God demonstrates his presence with them as a pillar of cloud and a pillar of fire. When Ezekiel is far away from home, God reassures him of his presence with a vision of a wheeled throne, showing that God's reign is equally present in Israel or in Babylon. When we travel, we prove in our experience that there is nowhere we can go from God's presence (Psalm 139). Strangely, it is often when I am furthest away from home that I feel closest to God, as though he is teaching me that it is vocation, rather than location, that brings intimacy with him.

God's mission

The fact that God's fingerprints are everywhere in creation and that God's presence has no geographical boundaries does not mean that travel is always the right option. Jonah is a great example of ungodly travel – he ran from where God wanted him to be by jumping on a sightseeing tour of Tarshish, rather than heading for Ninevah. Wherever you are thinking of going, make sure you are not running away from God's plans for your life. Nevertheless, God tells all of us to 'go' as his missionaries. For some of us that means heading into the city offices. For others it means taking that risky job. It may mean we go home, go to the other side of town or even to the other side of the world. Take a look at the motives, mission and mindset in the following reasons to travel, and consider where God might be sending you.

5 bad reasons to travel

1. Hedonism: 'After all the hard work at university, I deserve to have some fun and enjoy my freedom before work and family tie me down.'
2. Slum tourism: 'I've heard that from one hotel in India, I can take a coach tour around the shanty towns. I'd love to take some photos there.'
3. Consumerism: 'I've read the travel books – you just haven't lived unless you've ridden a camel in Egypt, been to Sydney Opera House and experienced white-knuckle rides in Florida.'

4. Escapism: 'I fancy good old-fashioned backpacking where nobody knows where I am – that will give me space totally to redefine myself, especially as I need to get some relationships out of my system.'
5. Defeatism: 'I haven't got a job to go to, and my dad doesn't want me coming home, so I'll just drift along until something crops up.'

5 good reasons to travel

1. To learn: 'I have friends I would like to visit, and they have inspired me with stories of what they are learning from the culture they are living in.'
2. To connect: 'I really believe God is calling me to serve his global church and open my eyes to the real world.'
3. To inspire: 'Life at university can get quite claustrophobic. I think it's a real privilege to be able to broaden my horizons and see how other people live.'
4. To praise: 'The Discovery Channel always makes me praise God more – perhaps travelling around the world for myself would have an even greater impact on me.'
5. To minister: 'I have made some really good friends at uni – they are planning to go round the world, and I really want to be with them and help them engage with the gospel as we go.'

 Further study: Read Jonah 4. What lessons are there about God's planet and God's people? How can we develop eyes that see the world from God's perspective?

 Prayer: Look at the first six days of creation in Genesis 1 and praise God for all he has made. Find some images online to inspire you.

> The proverbs of Solomon son of David, king of Israel:
>   for gaining wisdom and instruction;
>   for understanding words of insight;
>   for receiving instruction in prudent behaviour,
>   doing what is right and just and fair;
>   for giving prudence to those who are simple,
>   knowledge and discretion to the young –
>   let the wise listen and add to their learning,
>   and let the discerning get guidance –
>   for understanding proverbs and parables,
>   the sayings and riddles of the wise.
>   The fear of the LORD is the beginning of knowledge,
>   but fools despise wisdom and instruction.
> (Proverbs 1:1–7)

It's true – after years of sleep deprivation, empty wallet syndrome and a diet of macaroni cheese and Mars Bars, some people just want it never to end! Whether you simply cannot resist paying whatever it costs to prolong student life, or you are the sort of person who may as well be dating the library, postgraduate study, whether a Master's qualification or a doctoral degree, is often an attractive option. It could postpone any decisions to be made about career, or it could kick-start a career in academia. It could give you the edge over other applicants for jobs and promotions, or it could narrow down your career options. It can often be tailored to your own style and speed of learning and focus on an area that you are genuinely interested in, or it could broaden your education and teach you new skills.

I realized after about a week that I was useless at chemistry. My A levels didn't give me a lot of options, so I worked hard and did the best I could, ending my degree with what we used to call a 'Desmond' (2:2). I wanted to continue studying chemistry about as much as I wanted another hole in my head. Yet God hadn't finished with my studies – later I ended up doing a Master's and then a PhD in theology, going on to lecture at postgraduate level. I discovered that the rigour of postgraduate study can be very good for you – it can sharpen your analytical skills, help you to cut through the details to the heart of a problem, and recognize simplistic solutions or well-intentioned overstatements.

This chapter of Proverbs presents those of us who are considering a postgraduate course with three challenges.

1. Knowledge comes first and foremost from God

Wisdom is different from knowledge and information. Information is the presentation of raw data in ways that may have some useful significance, whereas knowledge is a grasp of that information and an ability to understand what it means. But wisdom is the skill or art of accessing information, applying knowledge and making good decisions for doing what is 'right and just and fair'. In this undervalued book of the Bible, Solomon passes on his God-given wisdom. He tells us that the key to this is humility, recognizing God's supremacy in all things. It makes sense at many levels – God as the only omniscient being in the universe and as the designer of the universe has a unique authority. But God is also the one for whom the universe exists, and so God's purposes are the key to understanding our lives and how they relate to everything else. However we choose to continue our learning, we are encouraged to check that we are pursuing wisdom by sitting at the feet of God, our teacher.

2. Knowledge goes together with prudence, discretion and discipline

Ironically, although humility before God is the key to true knowledge and wisdom, our limited knowledge can puff us up and give us a superiority complex (1 Corinthians 8:1–2). Godly knowledge should not lead to an inflated ego, but to a growing likeness to the prudence, discretion and discipline of Jesus. In this passage from Proverbs, too, we see that growing in head knowledge needs to be accompanied by growing godliness of our heart and actions.

3. Knowledge leads to action and justice

For Solomon, being a wise king was not just about ambition and reputation. He wanted to make sure his subjects were treated well, and the Bible records the fact that they were 'as numerous as the sand on the seashore; they ate, they drank and they were happy' (1 Kings 4:20). This begs the question of whether we are motivated to achieve a higher level of education primarily for a higher level of pay or respect, or for a higher level of responsibility or impact on society around us.

Postgraduate study may bring with it the temptation to become puffed up, to opt out of work and taxpaying, to become more acutely ambitious, or to be pulled further into debt or more reliant on our parents. But on the other hand, it may be a brilliant opportunity to glorify God with our minds, to be good stewards of our academic abilities, to exert greater influence over our institutions, businesses and countries, to deepen relationships at university with our peers and to develop critical thinking skills that can be useful in all of life. Whether or not we decide to pursue further study, it is helpful to note that Solomon's wisdom in the book of Proverbs encourages us to be lifelong learners.

In what ways have you already found studying to be rewarding? How have you also developed the following at university? Think of some practical examples for each one.

- prudence (being cautious with your resources)
- discipline (being controlled with your responsibilities)
- discretion (being considerate with your relationships)

Further study: Read Acts 22:1–5 and compare it with Philippians 3:1–9. How did Paul's excellent academic credentials help and hinder his ministry? What can we learn from his attitude?

Prayer: 'Instruct the wise and they will be wiser still; teach the righteous and they will add to their learning. The fear of the LORD is the beginning of wisdom, and knowledge of the Holy One is under-standing' (Proverbs 9:9–10). Ask God to show you how to become wise.

Having read theology, I thought I wanted to be a Bible teacher, so I decided to continue my studies and do an MA at London School of Theology. At the same time, the Director General of the Evangelical Alliance decided that he needed a research assistant to help prepare him for all the media opportunities that he was getting. A mutual friend suggested to him that he ask me, which he did, so I spent the next couple of years doing my MA part-time and working for him part-time. It was ideal! Ruth

'All the king's officials and the people of the royal provinces know that for any man or woman who approaches the king in the inner court without being summoned the king has but one law: that they be put to death unless the king extends the gold sceptre to them and spares their lives. But thirty days have passed since I was called to go to the king.'

When Esther's words were reported to Mordecai, he sent back this answer: 'Do not think that because you are in the king's house you alone of all the Jews will escape. For if you remain silent at this time, relief and deliverance for the Jews will arise from another place, but you and your father's family will perish. And who knows but that you have come to royal position for such a time as this?'

Then Esther sent this reply to Mordecai: 'Go, gather together all the Jews who are in Susa, and fast for me. Do not eat or drink for three days, night or day. I and my attendants will fast as you do. When this is done, I will go to the king, even though it is against the law. And if I perish, I perish.'
(Esther 4:11–16)

Jenny went to university on a teacher training course, but left with a degree in archaeology. She began a career in archaeology, but ended up back in teaching. So she trained to do an English language teaching course and ended up teaching in Greece, where she also got stuck in on a few archaeological digs. On returning to England she was totally confused. Whenever she was teaching, she wanted to be outside in the fresh air. But whenever she was out on an expedition, she missed the banter of school life. In her estimation she was a walking contradiction and a double failure. Or was she, as her friends told her, twice as employable with completely different options that suited her seasonal mood swings? With the average working adult changing career at least three times in their life, Jenny may be better equipped than most. So how do we handle making a career plan, but also bear in mind that God might call us to change that plan completely at some point? Is it worth doing a second degree or retraining in a totally different area straight after university?

One person in the Bible who changed career at least three times was Esther. After a difficult start in life as a Jewish refugee orphan, her first career was as a supermodel. Her outstanding beauty even caught the eye of the king, and since he had had his previous wife banished for disrespect, he eventually made Esther queen. It was during this second career that Esther was faced with a dilemma. She discovered that because her foster father had refused to honour Haman, the king's chief advisor, Haman had manipulated the king into issuing an edict to exterminate all the Jews in the kingdom. Esther's choice was simple: to stand back and watch the wiping out of her people and risk someone discovering that she too was a secret Jewess, or to stand up to the king in a third career move to diplomat and saviour, risking her own life in the process. We can learn something from Esther's decision-making that can be applied to those of us who are facing the quandary of whether to retrain in a totally different field.

1. Esther sought out advice

Esther undoubtedly lost a great deal of beauty sleep as she worried about the plight of her people. But rather than worry alone, she managed to get hold of the father figure in her life who had taken care of her as a child and who had not abandoned her when she became queen. Mordecai continued to watch her back by keeping his eyes and ears open from his vantage point at the king's gate. He loved Esther and he loved God and was able to offer godly advice. Mordecai had a profound understanding of God's will. He knew that nothing could happen outside of God's plans, and yet he also knew that God's people were responsible for doing the right thing. For those of us making decisions this is liberating and challenging. Whatever we decide, God's plan for the universe will not get messed up. But often it takes a lot of guts for us to do the right thing, and risk everything.

2. Esther was challenged to do the right thing

I doubt that Esther growing up as an orphan child had a specific career plan to be a supermodel-turned-queen-turned-national heroine. And this challenges us that God may have a far greater plan for our lives than we dare imagine. Mordecai had to remind Esther of this. He was sure about God's will, but whether Esther was the key to the salvation of the Jews at this time Mordecai did not know. Nevertheless, Mordecai challenged Esther to pursue her allegiance to God and God's people above her allegiance to her husband, the law and her career.

3. Esther decided to take the risk of faith

Esther sent word back to Mordecai, asking for his prayer support. The incredibly dangerous move of approaching the king uninvited was not something she could do alone. She even enlisted the support of her maids. Despite her successful career as a supermodel, Queen Esther had not become too big for her stilettos. She knew she was reliant on God and his people for the ability to fulfil her calling.

Throughout the Bible we see God helping people to change their careers. He turned Nehemiah the cupbearer into a wall-builder, a retired farmer called

Abraham into a nation planter, a shepherd boy called David into a king, and fishermen to fishers of men. It is not inconceivable that God is calling you to rethink your life vocation. Perhaps like Mordecai, you will leave your career to become a foster father or royal advisor. Perhaps like Esther, you will leave your career to take up a strategic position that may have life-changing consequences for thousands. This may happen when you are as old as Abraham or as young as Esther. It may happen now, during the final year at university. Whatever track we are on, the question is whether we are prepared to move if called, or take risks if necessary for the sake of God's kingdom.

 If you were to become a fresher again and do a second degree, what would you do differently? What advice would you give yourself?

 Further study: Read Judges 6. Here is a story about a breadmaker-turned-warrior; a wheat thresher-turned-Midianite thrasher. Why was it so hard for Gideon to come to terms with his career change? How did God show patience and persistence with Gideon?

 Prayer: What are the biggest problems facing this planet today? I can imagine Mordecai saying to you, 'Who knows but that you are about to graduate . . . for such a time as this?' Talk to God about your willingness to do something significant for him.

I was a Christian MP in the Labour Party when we decided to go to war in Iraq. I felt this was a spiritual issue, and I couldn't remain in my role as a Parliamentary Private Secretary, so I resigned on a matter of conscience. Some say it was career suicide – but I felt I had to honour God first with my job, whatever the consequences. Andy

> Daniel then said to the guard whom the chief official had appointed over Daniel, Hananiah, Mishael and Azariah, 'Please test your servants for ten days: give us nothing but vegetables to eat and water to drink. Then compare our appearance with that of the young men who eat the royal food, and treat your servants in accordance with what you see.' So he agreed to this and tested them for ten days.
>
> At the end of the ten days they looked healthier and better nourished than any of the young men who ate the royal food. So the guard took away their choice food and the wine they were to drink and gave them vegetables instead.
>
> To these four young men God gave knowledge and understanding of all kinds of literature and learning. And Daniel could understand visions and dreams of all kinds.
>
> At the end of the time set by the king to bring them into his service, the chief official presented them to Nebuchadnezzar. The king talked with them, and he found none equal to Daniel, Hananiah, Mishael and Azariah; so they entered the king's service. In every matter of wisdom and understanding about which the king questioned them, he found them ten times better than all the magicians and enchanters in his whole kingdom.
>
> (Daniel 1:11–20)

When I was at university, there was a popular joke along the lines of 'What do you say to an arts graduate with a job?' Answer: 'Burger and fries please.' While those with teaching degrees went into teaching, and those with engineering jobs found work at engineering companies, students with a qualification in Latin American studies or Classical Civilization were often the ones who found job fairs more challenging. On the other hand, a year later they were arguably the ones with the most interesting jobs, even if a small proportion were reduced to serving in fast food restaurants.

The predictability of Burger King is not a bad illustration of the student-graduate-employee conveyer belt in general. I know that when I walk through the door I will order a Whopper Meal, hand over my fiver, choose a seat, eat whilst texting, dispose of my copious amounts of packaging, thank the lady who is sweeping under my table and leave feeling I have just shortened my life expectancy by a week, and then I'll go in search of some chocolate to remove the aftertaste. Life can be similarly predictable: you go to school, sixth form, university, hand over your life savings, attend a couple of lectures, write a few essays, thank the person who hands you a certificate, and then accept the first job you are offered and live with the consequences.

The story of Daniel is a challenge to those of us looking for a graduate job to ensure that it is more than a conveyer-belt decision. Daniel was one of hundreds of bright young men conscripted onto a mass civil service training scheme. The authorities were planning on training and effectively transforming these noble Jewish boys to become good Babylonian men. But Daniel refused to play along, and it is his resistance to sell his soul that may help us decide how we approach the jobseeker's route.

1. A request

Daniel must have had some inkling that taking the king's choice food and wine would bring trouble. Perhaps he would have felt indebted to the king; perhaps he would have acclimatized to the trappings of luxurious Babylonian lifestyle. Maybe it would have numbed his ache for his home, his people and his God. So Daniel and his friends requested a diet of cabbage and water in order not to sell out. It may be tempting for us as debt-laden students to look through a list of opportunities and turn first to the salary figures, the holidays, the job title or the perks, but we may need to take a different approach to protect our souls and say no to these things in order to stay faithful to God in the marketplace.

2. A risk

Daniel took a risk in resisting the King's Burgers, and choosing the salad instead. And God rewarded Daniel with ten times the abilities of the other graduates. Perhaps that experience enabled Daniel and his friends to go on to take even greater risks. We see that after graduation Shadrach, Meschach and Abednego refused to bow to pressure from above or peer pressure when faced with a choice between worshipping God or a ninety-foot statue, and this resulted in the fiery furnace episode. And then Daniel would not allow his private devotional life be overrun by his work demands, despite running the risk of becoming the lions' supper. Whatever decisions we make at this stage – to go with or against the flow – will set a standard for our working lives. If we decide on our principles at this early stage, it will make it easier to resist losing our integrity when we are in the workplace.

3. A result

When Daniel had his interview, the king was taken aback by the outstanding applicant. Daniel was not in the privileged position of being able to choose which jobs to apply for or accept, but the role in which he was placed was not simply the foregone conclusion of the conveyer-belt training programme. Daniel could know that God had guided him into this position, and that by making godly choices he was learning to trust in God's faithfulness and prepare himself for workplace pressures.

Consider the choices and temptations we may face in preparing ourselves for our jobs: whether or not to work hard on our courses, whether to oversell ourselves on our CV, whether to apply for a job in a company with an unethical reputation, etc. It may be in these decisions that God guides us into the right job.

 Daniel made three good friends on his training course who stuck with him and kept in touch after graduation. Who are your 'Shadrach, Meschach and Abednego' who will help you take risks to protect your soul on the job?

 Further study: Read Colossians 3:23–24. Talk to Christians in the workplace to find out how they apply this principle on a regular basis.

 Prayer: Ephesians 2:10 tells us that God has prepared good works for us to do. Pray that you would discover those good works in the jobs and workplaces you go to.

Just before I left uni I felt strongly that God was telling me to beware of becoming dependent on middle-class comforts (worldly security) rather than on him. I spent my first months at work feeling tired (and couldn't work out how people managed to work eight hours a day with just one break for lunch). I was surprised to find myself resenting my employer for taking forty hours of my time – I guess that's why they pay you! However, it wasn't all bad, and I found it fascinating trying to work out the rules of the new game called 'work' – totally unlike academia, but if you played well, you could make the rules up yourself. Jeremy

A third time the LORD called, 'Samuel!' And Samuel got up and went to Eli and said, 'Here I am; you called me.'

Then Eli realised that the LORD was calling the boy. So Eli told Samuel, 'Go and lie down, and if he calls you, say, "Speak, LORD, for your servant is listening."' So Samuel went and lay down in his place.

The LORD came and stood there, calling as at the other times, 'Samuel! Samuel!'

Then Samuel said, 'Speak, for your servant is listening.'

And the LORD said to Samuel: 'See, I am about to do something in Israel that will make the ears of everyone who hears about it tingle. At that time I will carry out against Eli everything I spoke against his family – from beginning to end. For I told him that I would judge his family for ever because of the sin he knew about; his sons uttered blasphemies against God, and he failed to restrain them. Therefore I swore to the house of Eli, "The guilt of Eli's house will never be atoned for by sacrifice or offering."'

Samuel lay down until morning and then opened the doors of the house of the LORD. He was afraid to tell Eli the vision, but Eli called him and said, 'Samuel, my son.'

Samuel answered, 'Here I am.'

'What was it he said to you?' Eli asked. 'Do not hide it from me. May God deal with you, be it ever so severely, if you hide from me any-thing he told you.' So Samuel told him everything, hiding nothing from him. Then Eli said, 'He is the LORD; let him do what is good in his eyes.'
(1 Samuel 3:8–18)

The TV show *The Apprentice* offers much more than an hour of weekly enter-tainment, some great one-liners and a single prize of being Sir Alan's apprentice

– it offers hope. As the contestants continually fail the most basic of tasks, we enjoy the feeling that we ourselves are much more employable than we thought we were. However, despite the popularity of the show, apprenticeships and voluntary work are not often considered as serious options for graduates. Volunteer work is sometimes seen as something for the elderly or unemployable, but as Christians we are told, 'Freely you have received, freely give' (Matthew 10:8), and voluntary service is an obvious way to fulfil this command.

But there are other good reasons to consider this option. Whether in art galleries or in gardens, working with politicians or plumbers, in drop-in centres or special needs schools, the scope for personal development is enormous, and in return for offering time and effort, extra skills and experience will certainly be gained that will benefit any CV. On top of that is the bonus knowledge that you are contributing something to society. On the negative side, financial return is minimal, if not absent altogether – although it is probably cheaper than travelling round the world! The option is probably most attractive to students who take up an apprenticeship in return for a basic allowance, or are marrying a wage-earner, or have enough savings to live off, or are living at home, or whose natural job markets are saturated, or who are willing to work flexitime to fund themselves, or feel they have a definite calling into an industry where this is a necessary way in.

Voluntary work is not just a last resort option, as this story of Samuel illustrates. Samuel's work in the temple involved the mundane tasks of opening the doors, turning out the lights, and passing visually impaired Eli the priest the correct outfit. But whilst Samuel was offering his services free of charge, albeit in return for food, shelter and education, God was working something significant into his life.

1. Samuel learned from his mentor

Many volunteers often approach their work with the attitude that they will stick at it while they enjoy it, but if it turns into anything like hard work, they are free to take it or leave it. Samuel, on the other hand, seems to have been an eager learner, and Eli a good mentor. Even in the middle of the night Samuel is prepared to get up and help when summoned. And Eli, despite having been woken up twice already, is prepared to give Samuel some welcome spiritual and practical advice.

2. Samuel learned from God

Samuel did as Eli advised and heard God's voice speaking to him for the first time. But it wasn't a pleasant message. Eli may have been a good mentor, but as a father he had failed to discipline his two sons for greedily defiling the temple sacrifices. This was not the only time in history that an office junior has discovered corruption higher up in an organization, and wondered what to do with that information.

3. Samuel discovered his vocation

So when the temple opened to the public the next morning, Samuel opened up to Eli, leaving nothing out, although Eli had actually heard it all before in the previous chapter. Samuel's future vocation involved speaking God's truth in the midst of corruption – little did he know that this was only the start of it.

As a volunteer we may think we are exempt from corruption, commitment or significant contributions to the places where we are working. But God may well have other plans. The lessons learned from this story inspire us to develop good relationships, listen to God's voice, and be honest, even if this means upsetting the boss or the apple-cart. By doing so, perhaps like Samuel we will not only give, but also learn, practical and spiritual lessons, and maybe even discover our future vocation.

 Make a list of things you have to offer and things you could learn by becoming a volunteer. If you decide not to work as a volunteer at this point in your life, think about a project that you would like to volunteer for at some point.

 Further study: Read Acts 20:32–35. How do we understand the balance between the need to work to be financially independent and yet live to be voluntarily generous?

 Prayer: Adopt Samuel's prayer, 'Speak Lord, for your servant is listening.'

When I returned home from college after three years, I was worn out in many ways and desperately needed a complete break. My plan was to take a three-month break, then move off elsewhere to start a new job. However, God had other plans. I was very quickly involved with the local Guides and an outreach club for 7–11 year olds in my home village. I decided to do supply teaching to bring in some money while I worked out what to do. Within two weeks of this decision I'd had a week's work! This made me realize it was what God wanted, so I continued. It's now four years later and I do four activities with kids each week on a voluntary basis. Supply teaching enables me to earn enough, and I still have time for my voluntary work, which I consider to be my real calling from God.
Ruth

> Then the eleven disciples went to Galilee, to the mountain where Jesus had told them to go. When they saw him, they worshipped him; but some doubted. Then Jesus came to them and said, 'All authority in heaven and on earth has been given to me. Therefore go and make disciples of all nations, baptising them in the name of the Father and of the Son and of the Holy Spirit, and teaching them to obey everything I have commanded you. And surely I am with you always, to the very end of the age.'
> Matthew 28:16–20

The look of horror that came over my career counsellor's face still haunts me today. It was as though I'd said I wanted to become a bank robber when I left school. I had in fact told her that I planned to be a missionary, and I was informed in no uncertain terms that this was career suicide and a waste of my intelligence. She didn't want to know that according to Matthew, Jesus' last words on earth were to his disciples to become missionaries. Her last words to me were to reconsider what the computer programme had spewed out – fish farming! As I shut the door I was convinced – I was going to be a fisher of men instead.

We must be careful with terminology here, because whatever vocation God calls us to, we all have a missionary mandate. We can be a missionary backpacker, a missionary Master's student, a missionary businessman, a missionary policewoman, or a missionary volunteer. Everywhere we go, at home or abroad, we represent God to the people around us. But for some people, the call is to be a missionary missionary! And many Christian students at some point consider following that call into paid or unpaid 'full-time Christian work', to use a term only slightly less confusing.

Full-time Christian work offers a huge range of jobs, from translator to youth-worker, administrator to vicar. There are Christian musicians, counsellors, actors, writers and fund-raisers. For graduate students there are many opportunities to work in churches or Christian organizations, not only as permanent employees, but also on a short-term basis, which may be an ideal way to test the waters. For those of us considering this option, we can find much encouragement in Jesus' last words for our first step of missionary service.

1. Disciples that doubt can become missionaries

At one level no-one feels qualified to be a missionary. Even the apostle Paul struggled with the huge responsibility of representing Christ to the world when he wrote: 'And who is equal to such a task?' (2 Corinthians 2:16). But the graciousness of God is on display here at the end of Matthew's Gospel. Even when the disciples come face to face with the resurrected Christ in his glory, we are told, 'they worshipped him; but some doubted'. Yet all the disciples were commissioned to go into all the world on Jesus' mission. It is not our ability that qualifies us for mission, but God's ability to use us and our availability to him.

2. Disciples are authorized to pass on what they have learned

My first step in full-time Christian work was to go and pass on what others had passed on to me at university. I became a student worker because I realized that this was an area of experience I could offer back to God, and straight after university was an ideal moment to do that. Jesus sends his disciples out to teach others what he had taught them over the previous three years – to disciple the nations. You don't have to be full time in ministry to be able to pass on what you have learned – it can be done at church or in our families or friendship groups. But if you have grown as a Christian at university, then giving back to help the next generation of students learn about Jesus and grow in their faith may be the right next step for you too.

3. Disciples are empowered with the authority of Jesus himself

To a beleaguered bunch of young men, some say teenage boys, Jesus gave a commission to disciple the globe. Some of their hearts would have swelled up with the enormity of the challenge, while for others their hearts may have sunk, as most of them had not travelled far and the nations were seen as dark and dangerous places. But Jesus promises to empower his disciples with his authority and his presence with them.

In the period directly after university you may find yourself in a unique position – without mortgages, job contracts, marital and parental responsibilities – and this might be your best chance to take up one of the many exciting opportunities for cross-cultural mission work. Serving the church in this way will have other knock-on benefits. Learning to have a global mindset will transform the way you pray, study the Bible, give, and serve in your local church for the rest of your life. Spending some time learning from and ministering with members of our global Christian family can help us to mature and shake off the dangers of a consumer lifestyle. Why not test out a calling by setting aside a short period of time for Christian service oversees?

 If all Christians are missionaries, how will the things we have considered today apply to whatever you are planning to do after university?

 Further study: Read Luke 10:1–24. Jesus sent his disciples out so they could test the waters regarding their future in full-time Christian ministry. What principles can you take from this passage that could apply to students doing short-term service to see whether God is calling them into this sort of ministry full time.

 Prayer: 'Ask the Lord of the harvest, therefore, to send out workers into his harvest field' (Luke 10:2). Whenever you eat today, obey Jesus' command to pray for missionaries.

As I ministered alongside a local church in a township in South Africa for a month, I understood more of the grace of God than I had known before. It was watching Christians in poverty-stricken circumstances give sacrificially to Christians in neighbouring Zimbabwe that really challenged me. The fact that we were the first white people ever to have stayed in that township was a big encouragement to the local Christians, as we were breaking down old barriers – and I was humbled by their appreciation.
Alexandra

> But Naomi said, 'Return home, my daughters. Why would you come with me? . . . Return home, my daughters . . . It is more bitter for me than for you, because the LORD's hand has turned against me!'
>
> At this they wept aloud again. Then Orpah kissed her mother-in-law good-bye, but Ruth clung to her.
>
> 'Look,' said Naomi, 'your sister-in-law is going back to her people and her gods. Go back with her.'
>
> But Ruth replied, 'Don't urge me to leave you or to turn back from you. Where you go I will go, and where you stay I will stay. Your people will be my people and your God my God. Where you die I will die, and there I will be buried. May the LORD deal with me, be it ever so severely, if even death separates you and me.' When Naomi realised that Ruth was determined to go with her, she stopped urging her. (Ruth 1:11–18)

When Zac came to his last year at university, his main anxiety was that his search for a godly wife had so far failed and time was running out. When Kala came to her final year, her main anxiety was whether she would get her wedding dress made in time, and whether she would lose those six pounds. Neither Zac nor Kala found themselves remotely able to concentrate on exams and decisions about jobs. Kala ended up married, but unemployed and mildly depressed. Zac enrolled on another degree to pursue his ambition of finding his soulmate.

Like Kala, it is not uncommon for Christians to pair off – or try to – at university, making the next step after (or during) finals become something along the lines of a wedding planner. Neither is it uncommon for Christians not to pair off at university, like Zac, although that often leaves people feeling concerned that they have been left on the shelf and nervous about facing the next step after finals alone. This passage has some interesting lessons for both groups of people. It is a story set around three thousand years ago, when the pressure to marry young was even greater than it is today, and it focuses on a widowed single girl called Ruth who was probably much younger than the average finalist.

1. Some things are more important than marriage

Naomi knew that Ruth's best prospects of getting remarried were in Moab, so she encouraged her daughter-in-law to return home where her family could help her to find a new husband. But Ruth was willing to put her commitment to her mother-in-law above her marriage prospects. This was no easy call, and the other widowed daughter-in-law Orpah was unable to follow suit. We have talked a lot about God's call on our lives in this book, and God's call does not always hang around waiting for us to get hitched. Ruth inspires us to forge on with our vocation, even if that means risking singleness for the foreseeable future.

2. Relationship is for life, not just for convenience

Ruth's promise to Naomi is remarkably similar to the marriage vows that are said in church today – two different people from different families join together and promise faithfully to stay together until death do them part. This is a huge commitment and cannot be taken lightly. For Ruth it meant leaving her country and her family and never seeing them again. For anyone getting married, there are huge implications for the future. No more first dates, no more doing whatever you want, going wherever you want. Now decisions have to be made together, and career choices, for example, have to be made in tandem and organized to dovetail. But this passage shows us that the bonds of committed relationships are not restricted to married people – singleness does not have to mean loneliness and isolation. These two widows demonstrate a love and commitment to each other that could set us a standard for our own commitment to friends and families.

3. God has a plan

When Ruth follows Naomi back to Judah, leaving behind all the significant people and memories in her life, she has no idea what God is about to give her. Ruth crosses paths with Boaz, falls in love and gets married, without compromising her promise to Naomi. The couple go on to have a significant place in God's salvation history as the grandparents of King David. It may be difficult for those of us who are still single to swallow this fairy-tale happy ending. We may hope for it for ourselves, but we may also struggle with the fact that it might never be. One of Ruth's descendants may help us here. Jesus, unusually for his culture, was a life-long single. When he once went to a wedding, and not his own, he did not sulk in the corner, mourning what he would never have, but rather joined in the celebrations, and even enhanced them by providing free drinks all round.

Doing the wedding planner stuff, becoming a parent and home-maker may well feature in our plans for the future. Perhaps it is not the next-step plan for after university, or perhaps it is the only next-step plan we have. It may well be the last thing on our minds. The story of Ruth helps us to be realistic. Sometimes, like Ruth, we have to face singleness, because of the death of a spouse, because of an overriding calling, or because we have yet to meet Mr or Miss Right. Sometimes the ache of singleness can make us depressed or bitter – we see that Naomi returned home to Judah childless and alone after the death of her family and renamed herself 'Mara' (bitterness).

Sometimes God enables us to choose or embrace singleness. He may allow us to struggle with singleness and the knock-on effects of that, or sometimes God will provide a spouse. But whatever happens, God is always there with a plan for our lives that has more significance than we could ever dream of.

 How does the story of Ruth challenge you with regard to singleness, marriage and vocation? How does God's overarching plan encourage you?

 Further study: Genesis 2:18–25. Discuss how God designed vocation to be a man and woman team effort. What does this mean today for the dynamics of coordinating two career plans, for gender issues in the workplace, and for roles in the church?

 Prayer: 'May the LORD deal with me, be it ever so severely, if anything but death separates you and me.' Ask God to prepare you before you make a promise like this so that you will be able to keep it faithfully, whether to a spouse or to a friend.

I went to a wedding yesterday again [fifth of the summer!] and the groom asked, 'Jess, why are you still all alone? By the time I get back from my honeymoon I expect you to have a boyfriend!' My vicar asked me, 'Anyone for you yet, Jessica?' To which his wife added, 'My niece cried herself to sleep at night until she was thirty because she was single.' A good Christian friend from church asked my mum if I was aware that if I didn't meet anyone at university, then statistically it probably wasn't going to happen for me. I thought I made it clear I was happy being single!
Jessica

'Your kingdom come . . . on earth as it is in heaven'

All the routes we have discussed are valid options for Christians in their final year, and several routes could be combined or overlapped. Plot a variety of routes for your own life through different vocations and locations, and fill in the boxes to describe the different possible outcomes for ten years' time.

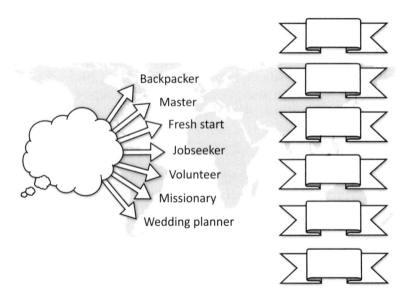

week 4

Anticipating the hurdles

Monday:
Applications

Tuesday:
Interviews

Wednesday:
Decisions

Thursday:
Rejections

Friday:
Finances

Saturday:
Tempations

Sunday:
Expectations

> Further, my brothers and sisters, rejoice in the Lord! It is no trouble for me to write the same things to you again, and it is a safeguard for you. Watch out for those dogs, those evildoers, those mutilators of the flesh. For it is we who are the circumcision, we who serve God by his Spirit, who boast in Christ Jesus, and who put no confidence in the flesh – though I myself have reasons for such confidence.
>
> If others think they have reasons to put confidence in the flesh, I have more: circumcised on the eighth day, of the people of Israel, of the tribe of Benjamin, a Hebrew of Hebrews; in regard to the law, a Pharisee; as for zeal, persecuting the church; as for righteousness based on the law, faultless.
>
> But whatever were gains to me I now consider loss for the sake of Christ.
>
> (Philippians 3:1–7)

I have had to type up my CV, fill out job application forms and write cover letters more times than I care to remember. But I have also been in the position where I have had to read through other people's job applications, CVs and cover letters. Presentation is a key factor, as is content, but unfortunately so is spelling. You have to imagine the hilarity in the office when the short-listing panel discover spelling errors such as 'poof-reading', 'party-time employment' or 'pubic relations'.

But apart from these sure-fire ways to get your CV binned, there are two other common errors we should keep an eye out for. The first is overselling ourselves, whereby we suddenly become fluent in the languages we only took to GCSE level, or try to prove that a two-week camping holiday in France qualifies us to be the managing director of a multinational tourist agency.

The second error is underselling ourselves, whereby we forget that leading a church youth group for two years is valuable experience when it comes to project management vacancies, or the fact that caring for a sick relative is likely to have built character traits such as loyalty, perseverance and initiative that a future employer would appreciate enormously.

CVs and job applications are supposed to be the way we advertise or market ourselves – in other words they are by very nature 'I'-focused. This can be dangerous ground for some of us, and unfamiliar ground for others. Some of us love talking about ourselves; for others it may be difficult to find anything worth saying. So here are three 'I's to help us keep the whole thing in perspective.

Identity

First of all, our CV cannot be the sum total of our identity. Paul, in his letter to the church at Philippi, wrote the perfect anti-CV. He listed his impressive family background, educational achievements and ministry experience, and then called them all a loss rather than gain. (In fact, the Greek is less polite – Paul said all of these accolades were excrement.) Paul wanted us to be sure that, although he could hold up his qualities and qualifications with one hand, he knew that it was important to be able to renounce them in terms of his spiritual credentials. Too often in the church we struggle to differentiate in this way. We measure people by their academic or professional success, and we create a virtual ranking system for spirituality based on achievement-oriented criteria. As we promote ourselves in the workplace, this passage is a helpful check to remind us that, although we can be proud of our CVs, our qualifications are not the basis of our acceptance with God. Paul challenges us to find our joy not in our achievements or our circumstances, but in the person of Jesus – not in what we have done, but in what Jesus has done for us.

Integrity

Secondly, our CV needs to reflect the fact that we are people of integrity. This means being as honest about our health as we are about our experiences of taking responsibility. It means that we ask our referees' permission before we put our CVs in the post. It means not being embarrassed by the fact that we won student of the year, or worked voluntarily in a children's holiday club. It may even mean we mention our faith if appropriate.

Inspiration

Thirdly, we need a bit of inspiration when compiling our CVs. Paul communicates with passion, persuasiveness and panache. Even in his anti-CV he shows a bit of a spark. We can make our CVs stand out with a bit of creativity, design and style, as well as with careful choice of words. There are many web templates that can inspire us with this.

Paul reminds us that we worship by the Spirit, and since the whole of our lives are supposed to be lived in worship to God, writing a CV is no exception. See it as an act of worship: thank God for the opportunities and qualifications he has given you; ask God to guide you to the right job; be proud of the person God has made you; and praise God that your life can glory in Jesus.

 Rewrite Philippians 3:4–7 as your own anti-CV.

Further study: Read 1 Samuel 16. Why would David's CV not have been shortlisted for the job of king under normal circumstances? What does this passage teach us about the most important aspect of our lives?

 Prayer: Are you more inclined to oversell yourself or undersell yourself? Spend some time asking God to give you a realistic and holistic sense of your own identity.

During the recession, job prospects were looking bleak for a lot of us, and most students who worked hard at their degree missed the opportunity of the jobs advertised in October and November. With the pressure of a career-driven society, everyone was trying to get into a graduate scheme, and one friend was reeled in by a scam she couldn't get out of. I felt stressed.
Steph

> But we have this treasure in jars of clay to show that this all-surpassing power is from God and not from us. We are hard pressed on every side, but not crushed; perplexed, but not in despair; persecuted, but not abandoned; struck down, but not destroyed . . . Since we have that same spirit of faith, we also believe and therefore speak, because we know that the one who raised the Lord Jesus from the dead will also raise us with Jesus and present us with you to himself. All this is for your benefit, so that the grace that is reaching more and more people may cause thanksgiving to overflow to the glory of God.
>
> Therefore we do not lose heart. Though outwardly we are wasting away, yet inwardly we are being renewed day by day. For our light and momentary troubles are achieving for us an eternal glory that far outweighs them all. So we fix our eyes not on what is seen, but on what is unseen, since what is seen is temporary, but what is unseen is eternal.
>
> (2 Corinthians 4:7–18)

The graduate was nervous as he rode the elevator up to the top floor. On his way up he used the gleaming metalwork as a mirror to perfect his hair, sniffed his armpits to make sure he wasn't emitting any foul odours, double-checked his fly zipper and spat on his shoes to give them that extra fresh shine. Turning to the girl behind him who was staring at her clipboard, he asked if she was feeling nervous about the interview too. As the doors opened she confidently told the graduate, 'Not any more'. A secretary approached and respectfully asked the woman with the clipboard if she was ready for the interview and invited them both into the interview room. As the woman took a seat opposite the graduate between two other panel members and in front of a label marked 'Head of Human Resources', the poor boy realized his mistake. He replayed his behaviour in the lift and his misjudgment of his travelling companion and knew that he would not be getting that job.

Paul reminds us in 2 Corinthians 5 that human standards of importance or social hierarchy cannot dictate how a Christian interacts with people. Skin colour, gender, accent, weight, bank balance or political power often influence us enormously, but Paul says that we can't afford to judge people in this way. His reasoning is outlined in the passage above, and can help us remember what God sees when he looks at us, and what are the true qualities we have to offer.

Treasure

When we go to interviews we can often feel as if we have to cover up what we are really like and put on a show of brilliance and confidence. This can be the beginning of a life career in charades where we project competence and disguise all weaknesses. But the Bible does not describe us as jars of clay dressed in treasure, but as treasure inside jars of clay. I was overtaken by a jar of clay on the motorway recently. I was speeding along at seventy mph when a three-wheeled Robin Reliant rapidly accelerated to around ninety mph and passed me with ease. The outer shell of this car, which would normally have only managed a couple of miles an hour if it was going downhill with a trailing wind, was hiding an expensive supercharged engine. I am often reminded of this when I read the Bible. Nobody would have guessed that scruffy baby brother David or smelly fishermen Peter and John would have been picked for the jobs they ended up with. God reverses the attitudes of the world, and this should give us hope – we are valuable treasure to be discovered by an employer.

Truthful

Being truthful in interview is more complicated these days because of Google! Many interviewers look up applicants on the web before an interview, which could make for some embarrassing moments. It's no use saying you are a controlled conscientious person if your email address is 'sexyanddrunk@HotMale.co.uk'! It's no good talking about how respectable you are, if you are tagged in compromising photos. It would be difficult for an employer to understand that you are going to be committed to the job if you have tweeted regularly about skipping lectures in favour of a lie-in. And if we have blogged about a mission trip, we shouldn't be surprised if we are asked about our faith.

Trouble

Interviews are some of the most intense experiences of our lives. Whether we are being introduced to the potential in-laws or interrogated by a future boss, or even investigated by a police officer, we need to think and speak on our feet. But it is not just our mouths that answer the questions. Whether we have dressed too smartly or too casually says a lot about us. Whether we have arrived too early or too late, sat too upright or too relaxed, said too much or too little, acted too confidently or too cautiously – interviews can feel like walking through a minefield. But it is when we are under pressure that our real character can often shine through; it is when we feel most weak, that we rely most on Jesus; and it is when we understand that our troubles are just 'light and momentary' that we look forward most to eternity with God.

The night before a big interview, I pressed my suit, polished my shoes and took out my hair clippers to make sure I was well groomed for the occasion. I asked my wife to help neaten up the back and sides and handed her the clippers. Two seconds later we both screamed simultaneously. Neither of us had noticed it was on the wrong setting and I now had a large bald patch above my left ear. During the interview I was so self-conscious, the panel must have wondered why I kept turning my head to one side and putting my hand over my ear. Fortunately they were less concerned with my physical appearance than they were with my potential to fulfil the job, and this has helped me keep a proper perspective in interviews ever since – as well as visit the barber more often!

 One of the hardest questions to answer in interview is about your strengths and weaknesses. How would you answer this? How does this passage counter any tendency to become heavy-hearted or big-headed?

 Further study: Read Revelation 3:1–6. What are the strengths and weaknesses of the church in Sardis? Where are they connected to God, and where are they disconnected. Assess your own spiritual strengths and weaknesses.

 Prayer: Ask God to give you clarity about your own strengths and weaknesses and to strike the right balance between boldness and humility.

I had applied for several retail management graduate training schemes, and got interviews, but unless you would agree to go anywhere in the country, there was a lot of competition for places, and in the Autumn term I was planning to come home to find work near my boyfriend. I think I scared the recruitment officers at John Lewis by wearing a purple trouser suit to my interview – at that time, their female staff all still wore skirts. Sarah

> Then Jesus went with his disciples to a place called Gethsemane, and he said to them, 'Sit here while I go over there and pray.' He took Peter and the two sons of Zebedee along with him, and he began to be sorrowful and troubled. Then he said to them, 'My soul is overwhelmed with sorrow to the point of death. Stay here and keep watch with me.'
>
> Going a little farther, he fell with his face to the ground and prayed, 'My Father, if it is possible, may this cup be taken from me. Yet not as I will, but as you will.'
>
> Then he returned to his disciples and found them sleeping. 'Couldn't you men keep watch with me for one hour?' he asked Peter. 'Watch and pray so that you will not fall into temptation. The spirit is willing, but the flesh is weak.'
>
> He went away a second time and prayed, 'My Father, if it is not possible for this cup to be taken away unless I drink it, may your will be done.'
>
> When he came back, he again found them sleeping, because their eyes were heavy. So he left them and went away once more and prayed the third time, saying the same thing.
>
> Then he returned to the disciples and said to them, 'Are you still sleeping and resting? Look, the hour is near, and the Son of Man is delivered into the hands of sinners.'
> (Matthew 26:36–45)

Homer Simpson somehow gets upgraded to first class in a flight, and when asked by a member of the cabin crew whether he would like one steak or two, he pauses a moment to make the decision. If you know anything about Homer Simpson, you would ask why the pause. This is a cartoon thirty-something who diets on doughnuts and beer, daydreams about chocolate, and drools over sprinkles. Surely there is no decision; surely he will take the plate of two steaks. But Homer is stumped because he doesn't want to choose – he wants both. This has become a family joke. Whenever there is a choice of dessert at the meal table, a choice of film at the cinema or a choice of drinks at a party, you can bet somebody will say in a Homer voice, 'D'oh, can't I have both?' Unfortunately decision-making can't always be so easily avoided by sheer indulgence; a choice has to be made.

Like so much of the Christian life, the cross has to be the place we go to get our bearings. The cross of Christ stands as a signpost for the Christian life. It says to us that we are acceptable to God in spite of our sin, that we are valuable to God irrespective of our finances, that we are loved by God regardless of our employment situation. The cross is the place where we make the most important decision of our lives – to follow the one who died in our place or do life our own way. The cross is the place where we come with all our decisions to check that our choices are pleasing to our Lord and Saviour. But the cross is also the place where we see Jesus model decision-making, as he faces the most difficult decision in all of history right under the noses of his disciples one black night in the Garden of Gethsemane.

Jesus' model

What happens in the garden that night is real, raw and riveting. Jesus is obviously in deep distress, sweating blood, sorrowful to the point of death, and seeking from his friends the simple courtesy of staying awake with him. Jesus is no mere cog in the atonement machine – he is wrestling with this decision to face the horrors of the physical torture and spiritual torment of carrying the sins of the world and facing separation from his Father. At the heart of his decision-making is the simple yet profound statement, 'Yet not as I will, but as you will.' Jesus models for us seeking first God's kingdom and submitting our will to him.

We are told to walk in the footsteps of Jesus, and nowhere are we on more holy ground than in the Garden of Gethsemane, not because the location is sacred, but because the vocation is sacred. To be a Christian means following Jesus, and that means with each decision we face in our career we need to echo Jesus' words, 'not as I will, but as you will'.

The disciples' model

We have another model in this passage. While Jesus was deciding whether to take the job of Saviour of the World, the disciples had been offered the job of prayer support. It did not appear to the disciples as a very important or urgent job. It seemed to them mundane, arduous and unglamorous – and it was a night shift. Their decision to take the job was far more influenced by their physical feelings than by the one who had asked them to do it. But Jesus very patiently and persistently lets us know that we need to turn this on its head – if God is calling us to a job, then we must rise to his challenge, no matter how we feel or what the world says.

When it comes to deciding which job to apply for or which job to accept, a cross-shaped way of living should be normal for us. This does not always mean that God will ask us to do jobs that are boring, difficult or dangerous – often God provides work for us that is satisfying and stimulating. But it does mean that he calls us to jobs that are part of his plan for the world. Honouring God first means that the final salary, the prestige or the location cannot be the deciding factor in our choice. First and foremost we need to lay ourselves before God at each stage of the process so that our decision has God's will at the centre. If this sounds too difficult, we can take comfort and encouragement from the words of Jesus, who sympathized with how the spiritual dimension seemed to battle the natural, practical and physical reaction when he said, 'The spirit is willing but the flesh is weak.' Jesus provides us with the example and the encouragement to obey, whatever the cost.

 Think about a decision you are facing at the moment. Why not take a couple of friends out to a park or garden at dusk and spend an hour in prayer together, seeking God's will.

 Further study: Read Genesis 13:1–18. How did Abraham and Lot make their decisions in this passage? What were the long-term consequences of those decisions? What can we learn from this story?

 Prayer: Pray through the Lord's Prayer in the context of anticipating decisions about job offers. Write down how it is particularly meaningful to you today.

I wanted my first year as a professional to be in a place where I knew the area and had friends, as I realized I would need the support. I considered whether my parent's town or my uni city was my home, or rather whether my home or uni church was my spiritual home. For me those ideas are interchangeable. I decided to stay near uni and looked for teaching jobs. I had to apply for forty or so jobs in the area before getting an interview though, and fifty before I got a job. God has shown me how trust in his provision and patience pays off. Fran

> But Zion said, 'The LORD has forsaken me,
>   the Lord has forgotten me.'
> 'Can a mother forget the baby at her breast
>   and have no compassion on the child she has borne?
> Though she may forget,
>   I will not forget you!
> See, I have engraved you on the palms of my hands;
>   your walls are ever before me.
> Your children hasten back,
>   and those who laid you waste depart from you.
> Lift up your eyes and look around;
>   all your children gather and come to you.
> As surely as I live,' declares the LORD,
>   'you will wear them all as ornaments;
>   you will put them on, like a bride.'
> (Isaiah 49:14–18)

I am a real sucker for competitions. If there is a chance to win the latest mobile phone with a soft drink, or a mini-cruise with my butter, or perhaps a small fortune with my cereal, my heart starts beating faster. My mind tells me that my chances are slim, but my heart tells me that sooner or later my big win will come. So I eagerly tear off the wrapper, open the lid, or rip up the box to find the code, convinced that the prize is mine and start planning all the cool things I could do with my winnings. Seconds later I see the word SORRY staring back at me, laughing in my face, and I am far more disappointed than I should be over what feels like another rejection.

Rejection comes at us from many angles: from having an online friendship request turned down to facing the fact that a birth parent gave us up for adoption; from being picked last for the netball team to hearing for the umpteenth time that we were not shortlisted for that job. Rejection can crush the human spirit, and make us feel less like a human being and more like a disposable coffee cup headed for the rubbish bin.

Where do we find the resources to pick ourselves up and start the application procedure all over again, tweaking our CV, filling in another form, swotting up on another company, putting on our smartest clothes for another interview and facing the wait for yet another rejection letter?

The Christian has a completely different starting point when it comes to rejection. Unlike other faiths, the Christian starts from the firm foundation that we are accepted by God. This acceptance does not ultimately depend on how we perform, on how well we live, on whether our good deeds outweigh our bad, or on whether we achieve karmic neutrality. It is based on God's rejection of Jesus. Because Jesus was pierced we can be healed, because Jesus was cursed by God we can be blessed, because Jesus was rejected we can be accepted (Galatians 3:12–14). This is the sure foundation from which every Christian starts before any other relationship comes into play, including any relationship with our future employers. It gives us an incredible amount of security and freedom. We don't have to creep through life trying to avoid rejection. We have been accepted by the eternal God and so, when earthly rejection comes, we can put it into perspective.

In Isaiah 49 we see the beauty of this in practice. Seven hundred years before the birth of Christ, Isaiah delivered a powerful prophecy from God. There had been a lot of bad news, as God's people had to face up to their idolatry immorality and their rejection of God. Yet despite the disastrous consequences of their rejection, God did not give up on his people. And as if that wasn't enough, he used the strongest language possible and a whole pile of metaphors, so his people would not only know in their heads that God accepted them unconditionally, but also feel it in their hearts.

1. Relationships

God's disciplining of his people by sending them into exile in Babylon made many Jews feel as though God had abandoned them. But in this passage God reaffirms his commitment to his people. Even if it were possible for a nursing mother to forget the baby she is feeding, God will never abandon his people. Whatever else changes in our lives, God can be utterly relied upon.

2. Plans

Rejection can cause us to become cynical about promises and plans for the future, but God wants us to know that he has tattooed us onto his hands – a permanent reminder in a place that everyone can see. With New Testament eyes, we can see that this is fulfilled in the nail-prints in Jesus' hands, made for us. We continually have God's attention and can move forwards with our lives.

3. Work

Rejection at work can cause us to lose heart and lose hope, but when God says 'your walls are ever before me', he is reminding us that he has not forgotten the job and the ministry we are doing, or the home and life we are building. God encourages us not to navel-gaze in despair, but to look up and look around and watch how God is bringing all things together.

God will never give up on us, and this should help us not to give up on our dreams and plans too quickly. Many of today's most successful business tycoons were turned down at interview somewhere along the line. The Beatles, for example, were turned down from numerous record labels before they were signed by Decca. On the other hand, we need to be aware that if rejection persists, God may be redirecting our future plans. Sometimes the Simon Cowell school of bluntness can help us reassess our own estimation of a particular career path.

 Make a plan to deal with rejection when it comes: which Bible passage will help you to voice your emotions to God? Which aspects of your character and plans will you allow the rejection to shape? How will you pick yourself up and wipe away the dust?

 Further study: Read Genesis 16:1–16. Discuss how each character in this story could have felt rejected. What did they do right, what did they do wrong, and how does God show his unconditional acceptance to each character? What can we learn from this?

 Prayer: 'The stone the builders rejected has become the capstone.' Quoted six times in Scripture about Jesus, meditate on how the rejection you experience draws you closer to Jesus, the rejected Messiah.

I had just finished a postgraduate diploma in management studies, having previously studied business and finance. It was a bit of a weird time, but I had fun with a mate wallpapering our lounge with the rejection letters. I think we got close to a hundred between us! Alan

Someone in the crowd said to him, 'Teacher, tell my brother to divide the inheritance with me.'

Jesus replied, 'Man, who appointed me a judge or an arbiter between you?' Then he said to them, 'Watch out! Be on your guard against all kinds of greed; life does not consist in an abundance of possessions.'

And he told them this parable: 'The ground of a certain rich man yielded an abundant harvest. He thought to himself, "What shall I do? I have no place to store my crops."

'Then he said, "This is what I'll do. I will tear down my barns and build bigger ones, and there I will store my surplus grain. And I'll say to myself, 'You have plenty of grain laid up for many years. Take life easy; eat, drink and be merry.'"

'But God said to him, "You fool! This very night your life will be demanded from you. Then who will get what you have prepared for yourself?"

'This is how it will be with those who store up things for themselves but are not rich towards God.'
(Luke 12:13–21)

Students can be quite creative when it comes to money-saving schemes. In his draughty student house, Dan used to wear all his clothes at once, and if he was still cold, he would allow himself a ten-second burst of his hairdryer down his jumper. Andy would use only one layer of the two-ply toilet paper, and Erin went for a swim each morning so she could get a free shower. Moving from learning to earning can be a huge relief for many of us leaving university, as we stop digging ourselves deeper into debt. But a new financial situation can bring as many problems as it solves, and it can expose the problems that were already lurking. Comic Jack Handey puts it in a deep-thought nutshell: 'When I am rich, I hope I am not mean to the poor, as I am now.'

Jesus puts it equally bluntly in the story he tells to the person known only as 'someone in the crowd' – an appropriate title as his request is surely not uncommon. As this man comes face to face with Jesus, he doesn't bow down in worship. All he can see is a possible solution to his messy financial affairs. But Jesus does not sink to his level; rather he tells a parable to explain the guy's myopia.

This parable is in some ways the opposite of another famous parable – the prodigal son. Here is a man who worked for his own money instead of cheating his family out of an inheritance, a man who is interested in sensible financial investments instead of blowing his cash on wild living. But in spite of all his wise economic decisions, God calls him a fool for his lack of forward planning. He had not reckoned on showing his accounts to God on his sudden death that night. Three things stand out for those of us anticipating a sudden rise in our spending power.

1. Be on your guard against greed

The whole Bible is full of stories of those whose greed ended in disaster. And for most of us they are lessons that we need to be reminded of over and over with each pay cheque or benefit payment that arrives. It can easily feel as though life is just a race to accumulate house, car, furniture, clothes, and more and more. Be on your guard.

2. Be generous to others

With each cheque comes the choice to spend the money on ourselves or on others. God's question for the successful businessman at death's door was, 'Who will get what you have prepared for yourself?' It seems to be his selfishness, rather than his judiciousness, that was about to get him into big trouble. When Joseph built warehouses to store the bumper harvest of the Egyptians, it was not so he could cosy down for a happy retirement, but for the welfare of the citizens of that nation and the foreigners in need. The Eskimos have a saying that Joseph would have approved of: 'The best place to store food is in someone else's stomach.' This attitude is difficult to maintain in the workplace where we are surrounded by people who live and work to provide for their own consumption habits. Nevertheless, the Bible challenges us with a very different perspective.

3. Be rich towards God

The story goes of two students watching a show about terminally ill patients. One turned to the other and said, 'Promise me that you would do something if I was in a vegetative state, unable to think and live independently. However much I protest, just disconnect all the machines, and throw away all the drugs – I would much rather die.' The other student promised and grinned. He walked across the room to the TV and unplugged it. Then he took his friend's iPod, Xbox, mobile phone, DVD player, laptop and cigarettes and locked them in his room. Finally he took the other guy's beer from the fridge and quickly locked himself in his room and wasn't seen for several days, leaving the first student dying of boredom!

That story should challenge us. Are we living with a loose hold on the stuff we have accumulated, even as poor students? Are we motivated now by financial rewards or the latest must-have? Are we generous with the money we have at the moment? Developing godly habits now is the best way to live differently in the future. How we deal with debt, windfalls, the parental back-up supply, budgets and giving may well become a pattern for our future, as we enter the world of taxpaying, pensions and mortgages.

 Spend a day fasting from one of your luxuries: coffee, beer, texting, chocolate. Think about where you would want that money to go: church, friends in need, international disaster relief, mission agencies, charities.

 Further study: Read 2 Corinthians 9:6–11. How can we learn to be generous, and maintain that attitude through the financial ups and downs of life?

 Prayer: Pray today for people around the world living below the poverty line. Look up some video about their struggles, and ask God to burn those images on our hearts to keep us mindful of others as we earn.

During revision for my finals, I typed up my friend's dissertation for £50, a fortune compared to my weekly food budget of about £12. I had my student loan in a savings account – this paid for my flight and some of the vaccinations. Savings, a small student overdraft and a few donations from family and church friends paid for my living costs for a three-month placement in Nairobi, Kenya. God taught me that if you can stick to a budget, and be faithful in supporting his work at home and overseas with the money he enables you to earn, he can do so much more with your time and resources than you could ever plan for yourself. Sarah

> The Israelites said to Gideon, 'Rule over us – you, your son and your grandson – because you have saved us from the hand of Midian.'
>
> But Gideon told them, 'I will not rule over you, nor will my son rule over you. The LORD will rule over you.' And he said, 'I do have one request, that each of you give me an ear-ring from your share of the plunder.' (It was the custom of the Ishmaelites to wear gold ear-rings.)
>
> They answered, 'We'll be glad to give them.' So they spread out a garment, and each of them threw a ring from his plunder onto it. The weight of the gold rings he asked for came to seventeen hundred shekels, not counting the ornaments, the pendants and the purple garments worn by the kings of Midian or the chains that were on their camels' necks. Gideon made the gold into an ephod, which he placed in Ophrah, his town. All Israel prostituted themselves by worshipping it there, and it became a snare to Gideon and his family. (Judges 8:22–27)

It has been said that today people worship their work, work at their play and play at their worship. When our whole lives become out of sync like this, it is no surprise that the fallout includes widespread burn-out and depression from overwork, a huge push towards self-gratification, a church that has little impact, and a weariness from withstanding temptation. This brief insight into Gideon's life may help us to realign our lives, determine our principles and be prepared for temptations that may come our way.

Gideon is every young boy's image of a great Bible hero. Plucked from obscurity like a young Luke Skywalker, he is just a farmhand who turns into a national hero. Who can't relate to his desire for evidence of God's call on his life through putting his fleece out and asking for the dew to be on the ground but not on the fleece? Who can fault his empirical mind that guards against a false positive by asking for the miracle to be reversed? But God isn't the only one being tested. God whittles down Gideon's modest-sized military strike force into a hand-picked crack squad of warriors who test Gideon's faith to the limit. The idea that this tiny band of brothers can take on the might of the Philistines and win against all odds through the ingenious use of false intelligence, distraction and decoys makes for a great bedtime story. But contrary to most Sunday school lessons, the story doesn't end there. Gideon's defeat of the Philistines is just one phase in a cycle of stories that begin with God's people rejecting God and reinvasion by God's enemies, followed by repentance and a rescue leading to yet another rejection. The cycle plays like a broken record in the book of Judges, and even Gideon gets caught in the groove, as he goes from leading the people to victory to being led astray himself.

If we can identify with Gideon's exploits in defending the faith, or with his commitment to bowing to God's rule at the beginning of the passage, then we should also beware that we may well not be immune to temptation, whether it be allowing ourselves to be lured by money, sex or power. Greed, immorality and idolatry are strongly linked together in the Bible, from the Ten Commandments to the book of Hosea, to this story in Judges. Let's take a closer look at how Gideon was ensnared by the values of the people around him:

1. It started with an ear-ring . . .
Gideon's faith helped him to turn down a job that was inappropriate, but this didn't guarantee his holiness. Sometimes when we are feeling most

confident that we are walking close to God, it is easiest for our feet to slip. Gideon's first error was to open a crack that led to the floodgates being unable to hold back the temptations. Our own experience tells us that the first lie or first crime is usually the hardest, so we need a zero tolerance in order to protect ourselves from crossing the point of no return.

2. It turned into an ephod . . .

There was nothing intrinsically wrong with the ephod – it was just another garment worn by a priest. But perhaps Gideon was kidding himself that the temptations he was allowing were in some way part of his Sunday best and glorifying to God. When we are going down the road towards temptation, it's easy to deceive ourselves that God won't know or wouldn't mind. But there are no pretences with God. In Gideon's case, the ephod was not just an ephod, it was an idol. We need to watch ourselves closely, as the smallest acquiescence to the world's values can divert us away from God.

3. It affected everyone . . .

What began as an apparently innocent request turned into what is described as the downfall of a nation as they reject God once more. Moreover, the passage also specifically mentions that the consequences were dreadful for Gideon's entire family. This is often true in office romances – they are difficult at the best of times, but when sexual immorality is involved, it is inevitably much more than a private affair. It affects the families of both parties, as well as those in the office, the reputation of God's people and God himself.

Principles can be gleaned from this case study as to how to deal with all sorts of temptations in the workplace. Our resolve should begin now, before we make even the first impression with our future colleagues, and while there are friends around who can keep us accountable.

How can we avoid greed, immorality and idolatry? Make some notes under the following headings of specific things you can do:

- Adoration
- Awareness
- Accountability

Further study: Read 2 Samuel 11 to see how David's immorality is very similar to Gideon's idolatry. How did it start, what did it turn into, and whom did it affect?

Prayer: Echo David's prayer for purity in Psalm 51.

Leaving university without having discovered your lifelong partner is very tough, especially for Christian girls. As time goes by, it's easier to find nice guys at work than at church, and you find yourself struggling to respect the boundaries you have always believed in.
Sara

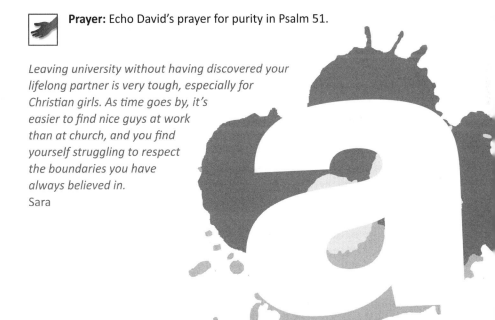

> Then James and John, the sons of Zebedee, came to him. 'Teacher,' they said, 'we want you to do for us whatever we ask.'
>
> 'What do you want me to do for you?' he asked.
>
> They replied, 'Let one of us sit at your right and the other at your left in your glory.'
>
> 'You don't know what you are asking,' Jesus said. 'Can you drink the cup I drink or be baptised with the baptism I am baptised with?'
>
> 'We can,' they answered.
>
> Jesus said to them, 'You will drink the cup I drink and be baptised with the baptism I am baptised with, but to sit at my right or left is not for me to grant. These places belong to those for whom they have been prepared.'
>
> When the ten heard about this, they became indignant with James and John. Jesus called them together and said, 'You know that those who are regarded as rulers of the Gentiles lord it over them, and their high officials exercise authority over them. Not so with you. Instead, whoever wants to become great among you must be your servant, and whoever wants to be first must be slave of all. For even the Son of Man did not come to be served, but to serve, and to give his life as a ransom for many.'
>
> (Mark 10:35–45)

I have never met a toddler who didn't gain an inordinate amount of pleasure from clomping through the house wearing her mother's shoes. Ten times larger than her own little feet and virtually impossible to walk in, yet worth the struggle as the grin stretches from ear to ear. And perhaps it is there that something begins. Sooner or later the child will take the next step of borrowing Mum's makeup, Mum's phone and Mum's car. But as soon as

Mum's shoes are the right size for the child's feet, she wouldn't be seen dead wearing them! Ambitions are elusive like that. We see in the workplace that ambition is a great motivator, but one that is never fulfilled, leaving us to struggle with expectations that can't ultimately be satisfied.

The passage tells of an occasion when the disciples were too big for their own boots, and how Jesus uses it to explain the new order of things for Christians. This speech by James and John reveals three common mistakes of people with misaligned expectations.

1. Over-inflated ego: 'We want you to do for us whatever we ask'

This is surely no way for two fishermen to approach the Creator of the world. They were right that Jesus was able to do whatever they asked, but wrong that they had the right to make demands of Jesus. Even before they made the big ask, they were talking to Jesus as though the position was already in the bag, and as though he were the genie in the lamp who existed only to do their bidding. Just as ambitious people can often tread on others on their way to the top, Christians can often pray for success at work as though they had the right to every job offer and promotion.

2. Overambitious goals: 'Let one of us sit at your right and the other at your left in your glory'

Their request is like asking to be given the bronze and silver medals in a race, or like wanting to be on the arm of a celebrity walking down the red carpet. They knew that Jesus was going to be powerful, and they wanted a part of that. The sad thing is that while they were wishing for some imaginary position in a future that they couldn't understand; they were missing out on the fact that they already held a position of enormous privilege. Christians around the globe have envied the first disciples for that intimacy with Jesus, for which we have to wait until eternity. The question for us as Christians in the workplace is not what we will do if and when we get to the powerful positions, but what are we doing with the privileges that we already have.

3. Overestimated abilities: 'We can'

Jesus knew that in order for him to be raised up in glory, he first had to bear the sin and punishment of the world. His question for his ambitious disciples was whether they too could drink that cup. James and John had no idea what Jesus was about to face, and yet with their eyes on these positions, they would agree to anything, despite causing disruption for their team. Power in the workplace is similarly deceptive – the more we want it, the more we feel we can and would do anything to get it. This is why it is said that power corrupts. Power can change intelligent and hard-working team players into insensitive, hard-nosed elbow-shovers.

In all our decisions and expectations for the future we should beware of the power of corruption and the corruption of power. While it is good to aim to fulfil the potential God has given us, we can easily become greedy or grabby, and instead of serving those around us, we can end up pushing them away.

 Spend some time thinking about your own expectations for the future. Does God fit into those plans, or do those plans fit into God's plan? How can you serve others around you through those plans?

Further study: Think about the following people in the Bible. How do we see them handle the temptations of power and corruption: Saul, David, Nebuchadnezzar, Daniel, Pilate, Paul.

 Prayer: Spend some time meditating on God's immense power and Jesus' incredible willingness to lay that aside.

Hopefully I'll be attending graduate school for PhD work in Political Theory/Philosophy so that I can become a professor. We'll see. Just gotta trust that my responsibility to my studies and God's providence will see everything come to fruition. But then again, why box God in with just one job possibility? Maybe I'll do something else cool. I'll take anything interesting (preferably with a pay cheque). I think. Who knows? I know how faithful God has been in providing opportunities and contacts for the future. I'm constantly amazed at how he works, especially when I got a dream summer job working for a Governor's speech-writer. Funny how God provides bigger than what we imagine.
Nick

'Your kingdom come . . . on earth as it is in heaven'

Think of some principles that you will stick to in the following areas. Divide them into positive principles – things you will do, and negative principles – things you will not do. Show them to a friend to keep you accountable.

	My positive principles:	My negative principles:
Applications		
Interviews		
Decisions		
Rejections		
Finances		
Temptations		
Expectations		

week 5

Leaving uni behind

Monday:
Consolidating friendships

Tuesday:
Communicating the gospel

Wednesday:
Committing to church

Thursday:
Contributing to the CU

Friday:
Concentrating on work

Saturday:
Coping with pressure

Sunday:
Clearing your conscience

Wounds from a friend can be trusted,
but an enemy multiplies kisses . . .
Like a bird that flees its nest
is anyone who flees from home.
Perfume and incense bring joy to the heart,
and the pleasantness of a friend
springs from their heartfelt advice.
Do not forsake your friend or a friend of your family,
and do not go to your relative's house when disaster
strikes you –
better a neighbour nearby than a relative far away.
Be wise, my child, and bring joy to my heart;
then I can answer anyone who treats me with contempt . . .
Take the garment of one who puts up security for a stranger;
hold it in pledge if it is done for an outsider.
If anyone loudly blesses a neighbour early in the morning,
it will be taken as a curse.
(Proverbs 27:6, 8–11, 13–14)

I'll be your friend – even if I have never met you before, even if I don't share a common language with you, even if I don't know anything about you. I will be your friend . . . on Facebook. Really – look me up and ask. Don't get too excited though; it doesn't cost me anything, I can't promise to read your updates, and I probably wouldn't recognize you if I passed you in the street, but I am very willing to give away this cheap friendship for free. I have to admit it makes me feel good to have a four-figure list of names of friends. I get to advertise books I think are good. And I also love the feeling of connectedness. I once had a very cool experience of being in a meeting of around

1,000 people, posting a photo of that meeting and within seconds hearing from a 'friend' in New Zealand saying that I was sitting next to his buddy Dave. Boy, could I have freaked that guy out! But although I can promise to be your friend online, you actually deserve better, as we will see from the Bible.

Whether you are a party animal or a net guru, the ancient sayings of King Solomon are remarkably relevant to those of us searching out friendships that will withstand the shock of moving from one common stomping ground to touring different worlds post university. Four themes stand out from this passage and each one is a worthwhile test of true friendship.

Loyalty

The proverb says, 'Do not forsake your friend or a friend of your family', highlighting a standard of loyalty that transcends the generations, and yet this is followed by 'better a neighbour nearby than a relative far away', implying that distance tends to limit our friendships, especially during difficult times. As we leave university this is the tension that we often face. If we are not careful, we can become nomads who tear around the country trying to maintain all of our friendships with the university diaspora, leaving no time to invest in our locality and becoming increasingly isolated and alone when we are at home. The other danger is to drop contact with our dispersed friends and thereby lose the opportunity for mutual accountability and encouragement from people who have come to know who we really are.

Learning

'Wounds from a friend can be trusted . . . ' We want our friendships to be safe and comfortable places where we can be sure we won't get hurt. But friendships that are willing to risk pain to be truthful are more valuable still.

We need the honesty of our closest friends to keep us faithful to God and faithful to ourselves. Proverbs 27:17 is similar: 'As iron sharpens iron, so one person sharpens another.' This painful sharpening process is actually a learning experience as other people help us spot our strengths and weaknesses, and investing in long-term friendships is a God-given means for us to grow to maturity.

Living

University may well have given us friends for life, but it has probably also skilled us for a lifetime of giving and receiving friendships, through intense community experiences. The Proverbs talk about our friendships in terms of real issues, whether it's an affectionate colleague, a nagging wife, a leery loan shark or a noisy neighbour. It is generally in eating, working and walking, as well as in tweeting, typing and skyping, that the nitty-gritty of daily life forms solid friendships. Taking the initiative to befriend those around us over coffee or over the garden fence not only helps us forge mutually beneficial relationships, but even more importantly allows us to demonstrate God's kindness, compassion and justice by living out our faith in those everyday scenarios (1 Peter 2:12).

Loving

The real challenge of this passage for me is not to find more friends, but to be a better friend. As Christians we follow the example of Jesus, who did not search out fellow carpenters, northerners or Nazarenes as his main friends, but drew people from all walks of life, became known as a friend of sinners, and laid down his life for those friends. Loving others the way Jesus did is still counter-cultural, but as we seek to give rather than to receive, we too will draw friends not only to ourselves, but also to God himself.

God has designed us to crave friendships and benefit from them spiritually, emotionally and practically, to mourn when friendships are broken or lost, and to celebrate when new friendships are found or formed. And so rupturing relationships when we leave university is bound to be difficult. But we can take our most important friendship with us: Solomon testifies to there being a 'friend who sticks closer than a brother', a friend the Bible will go on to describe as God himself, who will never leave us or forsake us.

 Take a friendship audit and check if you have friends from all walks of life. Then decide which will be Facebook acquaintances with whom you will try to maintain face-to-face loyalty, and which ones will help you to stay sharp and will ask you the honest questions as well as allowing you to return the compliment?

 Further study: Read 1 John 4:7–21. How are the themes of loyalty, learning, living and loving worked through in this passage in terms of our relationship with God inspiring us to show friendship to others.

 Prayer: Read Proverbs 18:24 and meditate on your friendship with Jesus. Speak to him as a brother/friend today.

In our second year at uni, a large group of us went out to a pub for some Christmas drinks and treated ourselves to a couple of bottles of port. Since then 'Port Night' has become an annual event, and every December we prioritize catching up with one another. It has been a brilliant way to keep up the friendships that were so valuable at uni. Susie

> Now the tax collectors and sinners were all gathering around to hear Jesus. But the Pharisees and the teachers of the law muttered, 'This man welcomes sinners and eats with them.'
>
> Then Jesus told them this parable: 'Suppose one of you has a hundred sheep and loses one of them. Doesn't he leave the ninety-nine in the open country and go after the lost sheep until he finds it? And when he finds it, he joyfully puts it on his shoulders and goes home. Then he calls his friends and neighbours together and says, "Rejoice with me; I have found my lost sheep." I tell you that in the same way there will be more rejoicing in heaven over one sinner who repents than over ninety-nine righteous people who do not need to repent.'
>
> (Luke 15:1–7)

I had made a bad mistake. In the rainy darkness I had turned off the dual carriageway too early and ended up on a works access road which was little more than a mud track with huge flooded potholes. I struggled to turn the unfamiliar hire car around in the tight space, but wheelspins and hazard lights were not going to help me blend back into the busy lane of a wintery rush hour. I was stuck – I was lost and I was late for a meeting. But I was not prepared to admit defeat. I was stubbornly determined to choose my moment and speed back on to the main road. Half an hour later I was still there, finally realizing that wiping lorry spray off my windscreen every few seconds was no way to spend the entire night. Embarrassed and humiliated, I phoned the police. When the flashing lights signalled their arrival ten minutes later, I expected some condescending confidence-crushing chastisement, but with a friendly and efficient wave, the officer in the patrol vehicle held up hundreds of impatient drivers, and graciously signalled me out, as though I was some celebrity who deserved the road to myself! Not only was I freed from my predicament; I was also freed from shame.

Being lost is extremely incapacitating and disempowering, making us feel stupid, alone and helpless, as I experienced that rainy night. But when Jesus talked about rescuing lost people, he did not focus on the mistakes of others, but allowed the impatient Pharisees to chastise him behind his back while he went out of his way to make those lost people feel important. Jesus hung out with them, not in a way that compromised his holiness, but in a way that corroborated it; and then he offered the sort of forgiveness and rescue that transformed lost people rather than humiliated them.

As we anticipate leaving university, we may well feel the urgency of wanting our lost friends to find Jesus. This is natural. If we love our friends, we want them to experience the same grace that we have come to appreciate. And if we love God, we share his heart to reach out and rescue the lost, rejoicing over each one brought home.

Some of us are honest enough to admit that we don't really feel that urgency, and this passage may help us grasp the pressing need of those around us. Luke, who missed out decades of Jesus' life story and incidents in his life, death and resurrection that other Gospel writers included, devoted a whole chapter to three stories with exactly the same message. This is Luke's way of writing in bold, underlining and then highlighting what he believes is the heart of his Gospel: God's delight when lost people come home to him.

1. Predicament

First of all the story highlights the predicament. A sheep without a shepherd is in as dire straits as a baby abandoned in the bushes. It cannot survive for long without someone taking responsibility for its care. Our friends may be oblivious as they cruise through life, but eventually they will realize that without faith in Jesus they are in big trouble.

2. Personal
Secondly, the story focuses in on the one individual sheep that is lost. Perhaps we get disheartened by the enormity of the job of evangelism at university, but if we can help just one friend come closer to finding God, we have done something significant for the kingdom.

3. Priority
The parable is clear that the shepherd has to prioritize the search and rescue mission over his own comfort and the daily needs of his flock, and he goes to great lengths to save the one missing sheep. When I was in my final year, I found it easiest to set apart a time for a seekers' Bible study one teatime hour a week. It was a priority in my schedule, but didn't distract me too much from the study I was supposed to be doing.

4. Party
Finally, the parable ends with a celebration and Jesus' echo of God's invitation – 'Rejoice with me'. Uni parties don't even begin to compare with celebrations that cross the divide between heaven and earth, God and humanity, now and eternity.

Our final year of university offers us a unique opportunity for evangelism. Many people around us will feel lost as they contemplate the big questions of life, meaning and purpose. As our usual means of spending quality time with these friends comes to an end, this parable inspires us to go to great lengths to reach out to them.

Which of the following could you commit to doing during your final year?

- spend time with the 'wrong' people – the ones least likely to look for God
- invite people for dinner/tea/breakfast on a regular basis
- invite people to church or a Christian meeting on campus
- run an Alpha/Christianity Explored course in your lounge

Further study: Think about the following people, and the different ways they led friends to Jesus: the woman at the well, Andrew, Zacchaeus, Philip. What can we learn from them about our opportunities in the rest of the year?

Prayer: Think about one person who you are desperate to see rescued. Ask God to help you go the extra mile for that person, to help you be bold enough to challenge them with the gospel, and to give you the privilege of leading them home to God before the end of the year.

When I was a committed atheist at university, I used to tell my best friend – who happened to be a Christian – that I thought the lions were right! Eventually I agreed to go to a Just Looking group to annoy him and show everyone up, but I found myself convinced more and more that the Christian faith was true and real. I had no choice: just weeks before I left uni, I began my journey with Jesus. Nick

> How good and pleasant it is
>   when God's people live together in unity!
> It is like precious oil poured on the head,
>   running down on the beard,
> running down on Aaron's beard,
>   down on the collar of his robe.
> It is as if the dew of Hermon
>   were falling on Mount Zion.
> For there the LORD bestows his blessing,
>   even life for evermore.
> (Psalm 133)

When it came to choosing a church when I was at university, I had three main criteria: good teaching, great music and great food. So when I turned up at a local church the first week, saw their amazing drummer, listened to the first sermon in what was going to be an eight-week series on Nehemiah (a book it took me ten minutes to find) and ate the best three-course Sunday lunch I had ever tasted, I was hooked. But there was a problem, and it affects most of us when we are choosing a church. Looking for a church that will satisfy my appetite for spiritual and physical food, and provide good music to wash it down, makes the church revolve around my needs. It turns me into a consumer and the church into a service provider.

The Bible teaches us about church in a completely different way. This psalm, for example, is not written to observe the weekly gathering of believers to sing songs and read the Bible, but to celebrate the community of believers sharing life together. This intimacy and interdependency occurs not only when life is going smoothly without any pressure, but is also arguably even more vital when facing the stress, decisions and surprises that the final year can bring.

To anyone who might think that church is a waste of time in your final year, this psalm is pertinent. At first glance, this passage could be portraying the epitome of waste. Precious oil is thrown away it seems. The guy is going to need a shower, a hair wash and possibly a new shirt. What a waste of time and money! But this case of spilt oil deserves a closer look, and the writer highlights four reasons to invest in church life through our final year and beyond.

1. Commission

The Old Testament introduces the pouring of oil as the equivalent of an ordination ceremony. Moses anointed Aaron, Israel's first chief priest, and Samuel anointed Saul and David for their role as king. We have to be careful to make a distinction here – the passage is not saying that church services are to be like ceremonies, but that the church unified, whether gathered or scattered, is a significant achievement to be celebrated. By implication, when the church is fragmented, whether due to disagreements between deacons, deans or denominations, or when people simply avoid talking to one another, the joy is gone. Many of us have experienced this, but by sticking with church we can aspire to unity despite the differences.

2. Consecration

In Exodus 29, God talks about the anointing of Aaron alongside the consecration of Aaron. Belonging to church will set us apart. It is hard to be different in this way, and we may well face criticism and persecution. But we, the church, are set apart for a purpose or a calling, just as Aaron was to serve the church. It may sound like a contradiction, but this is what God has called us to be – part of the body with a specific role and function, receiving and giving.

3. Source of refreshment

God did not specify the amount of oil to be used in an anointing, but there is certainly nothing sparing about the description here. The oil overflows, and a huge mountain of dew falls on the 'hillock' of Zion. However dry we feel spiritually, it is by being part of the church that God will pour out on us oil symbolic of blessing and dew symbolic of refreshment. When we are tired and stressed, these are the things we most need. Often we go to church expecting the people and the services to meet that need, and we leave feeling disappointed. But God has designed us differently. When we are active in pursuing unity, through resolving differences and serving the needs of others, God will pour blessing on us and those around.

4. Taste of eternity

The greatest blessing that the psalmist can think of is eternal life itself, and the church is a taster. Being with God and God's people, working together and worshipping him together is how the book of Revelation describes what we will be doing for the rest of our life. Keeping an eternal perspective often helps us when pressing deadlines seem to take over our entire life. But being a taster of eternity will also affect those around us. Our friends will notice when we prioritize being part of a church community. They will notice when we are offered a Sunday lunch when we haven't managed to cook a proper meal for ourselves for weeks. They will notice when we give up some of our time to babysit or move furniture for a family we know through church. Moving away from seeing church as a weekly dose of medicine, an obligation to fulfil, a spectator sport or a service provider, will free us to see church from God's perspective and enable us to stay committed despite disagreements, disappointments and periods of spiritual dryness, not only in our final year, but throughout the rest of our life.

 What would you say to people with the following comments about church?

- 'I'll get stuck in after my exams are out of the way.'
- 'I'm too busy with CU for church.'
- 'My church doesn't really understand the needs of anyone under forty.'
- 'Nobody really knows me in my church – it's so big.'

 Read the gory details in Exodus 29 and then the great deliverance in Hebrews 10:15–24. What does this comparison teach us about the importance of meeting regularly with God's people? Which of the four reasons to be part of a church that we looked at above are hinted at in the New Testament verses?

 Prayer: Phone or email somebody from your church today to find out prayer needs, and spend some time bringing these to God.

In my final year, as I wondered what to do next, God spoke to me one day as I walked past a tree in a London park. He pointed me to Jeremiah 17:7–8, which says 'Blessed are those who trust in the LORD . . . They will be like a tree planted by the water that sends out its roots by the stream. It does not fear when heat comes; its leaves are always green.' I knew that I needed to find a church in which to put down roots so that I could be consistently fruitful, even when life is tough, and not just when it's easy and fun. Pete

> You then, my son, be strong in the grace that is in Christ Jesus. And the things you have heard me say in the presence of many witnesses entrust to reliable people who will also be qualified to teach others. Join with me in suffering, like a good soldier of Christ Jesus. No-one serving as a soldier gets involved in civilian affairs; rather, they try to please their commanding officer. Similarly, anyone who competes as an athlete does not receive the victor's crown except by competing according to the rules. The hardworking farmer should be the first to receive a share of the crops. Reflect on what I am saying, for the Lord will give you insight into all this.
> (2 Timothy 2:1–7)

When I first decided to cycle the ten-mile round route from Marylebone to the Oval as part of my daily commute, it was a complicated business. I poured over the maps on the computer trying to memorize the route. I even programmed my TomTom and took it out at traffic lights – which got me some very odd looks. I ordered a cyclist's guide from Transport for London, I stopped taxi drivers for some expert advice and I went for the 'failsafe' trial-and-error approach. But it was only when I made a friend who was a skilled and seasoned city cyclist that I nailed my route. He showed me some nifty moves, off-the-map routes and short cuts that helped me avoid traffic lights, traffic jams, accident blackspots and bus lanes. I could probably even do it with my eyes closed now!

There is no substitute for having someone with experience show you the way to go, and as you look back over your time as a student, perhaps you have had a similar journey. Books, expert advice, the internet and trial and error can only take you so far, and I expect you could point to times when you have made mistakes or ended up down a dead end. You could probably point to a few people who have helped you en-route because they had been that way before. Whether you have gleaned wisdom at university by making the most of what was on offer or by making mistakes along the way, I would like to encourage you to pass that wisdom on to the next generation of students before you leave.

The chances are that the Christian Union was a real help to you in your first year. Perhaps it helped you connect with other Christians at university and gave you a safe place to wrestle with some of the big issues of faith and life. Perhaps the main meetings and small groups provided a sense of community and belonging, and the mission emphasis provided an edge to your Christian life. The following year the CU may have given you opportunities to lead things, serve on committees, take responsibilities, consolidate relationships, or take the next step in your faith. But by your final year, it is probably in the CU where you will be most able to pass on advice, support and wisdom to a new generation of students and student leaders.

When Paul wrote his second letter to Timothy, he was a finalist. He was facing not the final months at university but his final moments on earth, and what he focuses on is challenging to us. He was not trying to make his own exit a little easier by enlisting support to avoid decapitation, nor was he trying to focus solely on getting himself ready for the next port of call. Instead Paul turned his attention to the next generation – Timothy – to the generation after that – 'reliable leaders' – and even the one after that – 'others'. Paul's final letter concentrated on passing on what he had learned.

Paul wanted the life that he lived, right up until the end, to model something to the generations that looked up to him. He wanted his dedication to the cause of Christ, to pleasing his commanding officer, reaching the finish line and receiving his reward, to be more than a personal challenge. He loved to see others catching the vision in their spiritual journeys, and he challenges us to join with him in this enterprise.

Taking a leaf out of Paul's book should make us reconsider our commitment to CU in our final year. Even if we feel there might not be much for us to learn or gain from the meetings, there may well be something we can offer. It may not be formal recognized leadership, but attending meetings with the hope of encouraging, mentoring, inspiring and discipling others can have a significant impact on the next generation, and the one after that, and the one after that.

In his final year at university, John met me in a CU meeting and drove a ten-mile round trip each Sunday morning just to help me get to church on time – he wouldn't even take any money for petrol. Steve in his final year at university rebuilt the PA system from scratch and taught a couple of first years to be, as we called them, 'sound men of God'. Andy decided in his final year to teach a couple of first years to pray and study the Bible. Cath in her final year decided to come to the CU houseparty, not as a punter or a leader, but as a cook. These four finalists made as much impact on me as a fresher as the second-year executive committee – so much of an impact that not only did I continue supporting the CU in my final year, I then stayed two more years as a Relay Worker, which allowed me to see the results of that investment as rookie freshers went on to lead the CU, and CU leaders went on to be involved in mission projects around the world.

Paradoxically, this attitude of giving often means that 'it is in giving that we receive', as St Francis of Assisi famously said. How can this help us as we decide how much time and energy to commit to the CU in our final year at university?

 Further study: The end of the second letter to Timothy contains a list of names (2 Timothy 4:9–22). Many of those people left the ministry, it seems, whereas others helped Paul's mission. What can you find out about those people? How do these verses speak to us as we decide our level of involvement in CU?

 Prayer: Imagine yourself working as an athlete, farmer or soldier. What tasks do you see yourself doing? What would characterize your attitude? What would motivate you? Ask God to show you how you can serve him as a finalist in your CU context.

I stuck with the CU because it was about reaching the university and that needed to keep happening all the way. I knew that I could pass on my experience to newer students and learn from the passion of freshers too. I came, served and tried out new things – like finally discovering our international students' café, which was a brilliant opportunity.
Dave

God is our refuge and strength,
    an ever-present help in trouble.
Therefore we will not fear, though the earth give way
    and the mountains fall into the heart of the sea,
though its waters roar and foam
    and the mountains quake with their surging . . .
Nations are in uproar, kingdoms fall;
    he lifts his voice, the earth melts.
The LORD Almighty is with us;
        the God of Jacob is our fortress . . .
'Be still, and know that I am God;
    I will be exalted among the nations,
    I will be exalted in the earth.'
(Psalm 46:1–3, 6–7, 10)

Dear Mum and Dad
I am very sorry that I haven't been in touch for so long. I am getting along
pretty well now. The skull fracture I got when I jumped out of the window
of my residence when it caught fire shortly after I started my final year is
virtually healed now. Fortunately one of my physiotherapists offered for me
to stay in his apartment. It's only a small space but we've made it homely
and will live there after we get married. We haven't set a date yet, but it will
be after he is granted citizenship and before my pregnancy begins to show.
Oh and by the way, what with everything else going on this year, I am pleased
to report that I still managed to pass some of my subjects, but I will have to
resit the whole year.
Yours, Eve
P.S. Keep perspective – I am retaking my year – everything else is fictional.

In our final year it is easy to lose perspective about the importance of actually getting down to studying. On a practical level, our social life is peaking, we are in the middle of decisions about the following year, the end is in sight and the weather is improving. But behind those factors are three temptations that this psalm helps to keep in check.

1. Panic

I love flicking through worst-case scenario books. They give you all sorts of advice about what to do if you get kidnapped, or if you come face to face with a stampeding rhinoceros or end up trapped in a car that is sinking in a lake. Part of the enjoyment factor of these books is that no matter how bad my day is going, I realize that things could be worse, and even if they were a thousand times worse, there is probably a simple solution. Did you know for example that if on the way to your final exam you got your arm locked in an alligator's jaw, then simply by punching it on the snout with your spare hand, you could escape? The psalmist helps us override any panic we might be feeling with his own worst-case scenario – a simultaneous earthquake, tsunami and world war. Even this triad of terror will not shake his confidence in God as his refuge. With God ultimately in control of the universe, we can rest assured in two unchangeable facts – that he is with us, and that we will one day be with him.

2. Laziness

The equal and opposite danger for Christian students is to think that because God has got it all worked out we don't need to bother to do anything: it doesn't matter if we fail our exams or hand in an essay late, we can just chill out and enjoy the ride. We could even try to justify it from this passage when we are told to be still and know that God is God. But the context in this passage is being calm in the midst of calamity, not being lazy on the job. Jesus told us to seek his kingdom, the New Jerusalem, to be peacemakers, and to love God with all of our heart, mind and strength. So in confident assurance of God's final victory, we live actively, hopefully and passionately now, whatever the circumstances in whatever we do.

3. Distraction

While I was revising in the library, I realized that a librarian went around with a clicker at the same time each day counting the people in the building. So a group of us planned a caper. Since there were various routes between the floors, we decided to try to get clicked on every floor of the library without raising suspicions. It took some intricate planning, schematic diagrams, and the use of service elevators and back staircases. It obviously took up far more time than we had available – all for a five-minute prank that didn't even make it into the student rag. But when you are supposed to be revising, any distraction seems welcome and unnaturally attractive. We may need someone to help us spot the difference between a valid and invalid distraction. The psalmist had learned to recognize the difference and knew that it was God's kingdom that would ultimately last, and God's presence that enabled him to keep perspective.

On a practical level, there are lots of tested methods and practical advice to help us stay focused. Aim for a balanced life. Eat, drink and sleep regularly. Work in short blocks. Perhaps the variety of study, revision and job applications will help to relieve the monotony of concentrating on just one. Talk through what you are learning with a colleague and use memory aids. Try to complete assignments ahead of time and speak to your tutor if you are struggling.

Use the following grid to help you prioritize aspects of your life. For example, inviting your sister to come and stay may be important but not urgent. Buying a pint of milk may be urgent but not important.

	Urgent	Not urgent
Important	1	2
Not important	3	4

 Further study: Memorize Colossians 3:23–24 and think of some practical applications.

 Prayer: Finish these sentences in your own words: 'Therefore we will not fear, though . . . '/'Be still and know that . . . ' Declare this new psalm.

It was so easy to get distracted from music college work when I was wrestling with health problems, planning a wedding, running a small CU and playing in as many concerts and competitions as I could, but God graciously pulled me through.
Lois

> When Jesus heard what had happened, he withdrew by boat privately to a solitary place. Hearing of this, the crowds followed him on foot from the towns. When Jesus landed and saw a large crowd, he had compassion on them and healed those who were ill.
>
> As evening approached, the disciples came to him and said, 'This is a remote place, and it's already getting late. Send the crowds away, so they can go to the villages and buy themselves some food.'
>
> Jesus replied, 'They do not need to go away. You give them something to eat.'
>
> 'We have here only five loaves of bread and two fish,' they answered.
>
> 'Bring them here to me,' he said. And he told the people to sit down on the grass. Taking the five loaves and the two fish and looking up to heaven, he gave thanks and broke the loaves. Then he gave them to the disciples, and the disciples gave them to the people. They all ate and were satisfied, and the disciples picked up twelve basketfuls of broken pieces that were left over. The number of those who ate was about five thousand men, besides women and children.
>
> Immediately Jesus made the disciples get into the boat and go on ahead of him to the other side, while he dismissed the crowd. After he had dismissed them, he went up on a mountainside by himself to pray.
>
> (Matthew 14:13–23)

One stressed finalist, the story goes, after a night's heavy cramming picked up three pints of beer and was about to take them with him into the exam, when he was stopped by the invigilator. Not one to let his beer go to waste, the finalist downed all three pints and reeled over to his seat. While his course mates were busy covering reams of paper with long essays, he managed to write his name on the top of the paper before spending the rest of the exam asleep with his head on his hands. With the words 'You may now put your pens down', he woke up in horror to the reality of handing in a blank sheet of paper.

One exhausted examiner, the story goes, was marking late into the night, and as she made her way through one monotonous exam script after another, she too fell asleep with her head on her hands. The cigarette in her mouth dropped on to the mass of paperwork, and it was not long before she woke up to the sound of the crackling sheets as her work and the efforts of a hundred students were destroyed. And so it was that the student who had spent his exam drinking and sleeping was, along with his conscientious course mates, awarded a respectable 2:1.

This urban myth became a prayer for many of my atheist friends as they approached the stress of exam week. That week was an education for me as I saw first-hand what pressure does to people. The atheists pray, the cleanest people forget to wash, the gentlest people become irritable, and the strongest people become vulnerable to temptations they are usually well able to withstand.

When I lived on a busy street in London, I once saw pressure transform another whole community. The crashing noise of a multiple vehicle accident caused the neighbours to leave their houses and gather together on the street. People who usually never spoke to one another suddenly were not only being chatty, but were also caring, intimate, and generous. Some were looking after the injured or working together to extract bits of wreckage from the road, and others were making drinks for everybody. Pressure did not bring the worst out of us, as I had experienced before, but the best.

Jesus and his disciples were under pressure in this episode recorded in Matthew's Gospel. They had just heard that Jesus' cousin John had been executed, and the already physically tired team were coping with this additional shock and the implications for their own future. Jesus deliberately carved out some time to be away from the crowds, but they chased him down like a pack of paparazzi. How he reacted provides us with a role model to aspire to.

1. Jesus took care of others

Even at the most inconvenient time and even though the crowds were insensitive to the needs of Jesus, he nevertheless did not send them away or treat them as a drain on his resources. He saw their needs and he went out of his way to meet them. Even when we are most under pressure, following Jesus will mean that we still make time for the needs of others.

2. Jesus took care of himself

Jesus was fully human and fully divine, and as a human being he knew he needed time out. Before and after the feeding of the five thousand, we see him looking for privacy and a space to pray. We are designed to need time in our busyness for refreshment and recreation, and we are designed to find peace and perspective in our private relationship with God. So we shouldn't feel guilty about setting aside time for ourselves and time out with God.

3. Jesus takes care of us

Not only can we learn from Jesus in this incident, we can also identify with the needy crowds. We learn that Jesus is never too occupied to help us with our daily needs. He will never fall asleep on the job. He is never too busy with more important matters than the pressures we are facing. We don't need to feel that we can't bother Jesus. He welcomes us whatever our needs and he will be there for us.

Stress affects us all in different ways, and it is good to know how we react, where our breaking point is and what we can do to step back, calm down and stay sane and generous. The Bible doesn't promise to take away the pressures and stresses of life, but Jesus is both a hero to copy and a hero to carry us when our resources fail.

 Pressure in our final year often comes from the fear of failure or feeling that our self-worth depends on our achievements. How can that bring out the worst and the best in us? How can our relationship with Jesus help us through this time?

 Further study: Read the account of Peter's denial in John 18 and his reinstatement in John 21. Pressure brings out the worst in Peter; he lets himself and his master down. What encouragement can we find in this story that we can apply to our own situation?

 Prayer: Find somewhere remote to pray today. Ask God to give you physical, emotional and spiritual nourishment.

It's hard to see God's direction amid peer pressure, university pressure, and the currently imaginable or available after-university options. It's hard to keep ALL doors open to let God direct. I am often led by passions and situations, but unsure if that is God's direction or my earthly wisdom. Sonia

> For the grace of God has appeared that offers salvation to all people.
> It teaches us to say 'No' to ungodliness and worldly passions, and
> to live self-controlled, upright and godly lives in this present age,
> while we wait for the blessed hope – the appearing of the glory of
> our great God and Saviour, Jesus Christ, who gave himself for us to
> redeem us from all wickedness and to purify for himself a people
> that are his very own, eager to do what is good.
> (Titus 2:11–14)

Dorian Gray was stunningly handsome. No matter how old he became, he seemed to have the secret of eternal youth. But behind the polished exterior, Dorian hid a framed portrait that became increasingly deformed with each callous act. Descending into a more and more immoral life, he finally was forced to face up to the disgusting man in the portrait, and as his conscience got the better of him, he took a knife and stabbed the canvas. Hearing a scream, one of the servants rushed into the room to find Dorian Gray slumped on the floor bleeding out of the knife wound in his chest – his body elderly and disfigured beside a picture that was restored and youthful.

Oscar Wilde's powerful short story *The Picture of Dorian Gray* is a tale of substitution not unfamiliar to many of us who try to hide our ugly mistakes behind our accomplished façade. But we cannot sweep the dust under the carpet for long before the lumps and bumps reach the surface. Looking back over our student life will no doubt raise a lot of happy memories; but for some of us, there will be that sense of disappointment and regret at our failures. We may be leaving behind us relationships in tatters, a series of missed lectures, a pattern of falling into temptation, a compromised Christian witness or a debt that is out of control. We may be looking forward to moving on to the next step to put these mistakes behind us, but we are afraid that they have the power to catch up with us.

The Bible teaches that we can't expect to earn God's favour – nobody is perfect. We all make mistakes, act selfishly and forget God. But the problem that Titus' church was facing was to fall for the teaching that they could sin as much as they liked and get away with it because they had a 'Get Out of Hell Free' card up their sleeve. So Paul reminds us of another powerful story of substitution that can offer us a way out of the accumulation of sin and shame.

Paul says that Jesus took our place, 'gave himself for us' or 'redeemed us'. It is because of what Jesus did and the grace of God that we are made right with God from whatever state we have got ourselves into. Paul includes himself in this description – it was because of God's grace that he was rescued from a life of murderous religious intolerance.

I was rescued once by the British military. But a week after I was extracted from the war zone and returned home, I was shocked to receive a bill for services rendered. That is not how God's rescue works. This passage shows that the grace of God does not cost us a penny, but it should change us.

First of all, it changes our behaviour as grace teaches us not to make the same mistakes again, and also to replace negative ways of living with positive ones so we become more gracious and godly. Secondly, it changes our motivation, making us eager to choose ways of living that please God. Thirdly, it changes our identity, so we are no longer haunted by mistakes made in the past, but are transformed, purified and defined by God's ownership of us.

The learning process highlighted in this passage is not going to end when our academic learning ends. When God teaches us to lead upright, self-controlled and godly lives, it is a classroom we need to sit in for the rest of our lives until we meet Jesus face to face.

In our final year at university we may long for a fresh start for our consciences. But this will not happen automatically when we leave and make a fresh start in our career. God wants to help us wipe the slate clean now, turn away from bad habits now, put right broken relationships now and leave university with a cleansed conscience.

This is the final page of the final chapter of this *FINAL* book about what to do in your final year. But this is actually the beginning of the rest of your life. It reminds me of a day at the beach with Peter. He had failed his final exam, turned his back on his friends and his mentor, and reneged on everything he had believed in. And yet the grace of God shone through when the resurrected Jesus cooked breakfast for him on that beach, and then gave him a chance to resit his exam and sent him on a mission that transformed the lives of millions, including Peter's. If God's grace was enough for Peter, it will be enough for us as we launch out into the rest of our lives with him.

 If you had your time at university again, what would you have done differently? Make a list of things that God wants to redeem and purify you from.

Further study: Read Psalm 103. How do we see the themes of grace, redemption and transformation described in this passage? How does today's study inspire you to worship? How does it encourage you to retain your youthful hunger for learning from God?

 Prayer: Look back over your time at university and offer your regrets, mistakes and failings to God, asking him to cleanse your conscience and wipe the slate clean. Look back and thank God for the way he has guided and transformed you during your time at university.

Leaving uni is a weird experience – you're so involved in the culture
and community, so suddenly to stop is quite a strange thing.
But I'd say that more than anything it's an
incredible time of opportunity,
especially spiritually.
Dave

'Your kingdom come . . . on earth as it is in heaven'
This week's topics could be seen as seven different juggling balls that we have to keep our eyes on. What would it take to bring closure in each of these areas during our final year at university? Write in your ideal outcome for each area.

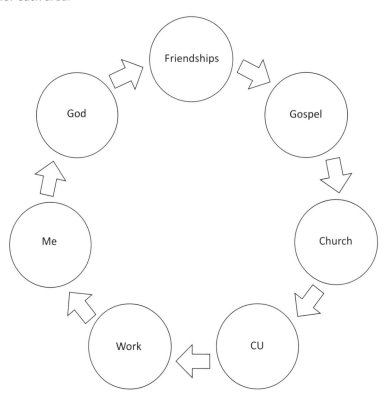